The Girl in the Chrysalis

the girl in the chrysalis

DISCOVER
YOUR UNIQUE SELF
&
LIVE WITH THEME
AND FLAME

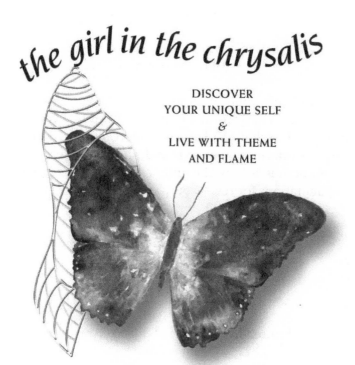

LYDIA WEI

**The Girl in the Chrysalis: Discover Your Unique Self &
Live with Theme and Flame**

Printed by CreateSpace, an Amazon Company
ISBN-13: 978-1979535656
ISBN-10: 1979535655
LCCN: 2017917402

Printed in the United States of America
First Edition

Cover: Desimone Design
Illustration: Lisa Salan
Photo of author: Dan Chen

Dedication

To my precious daughters

 Audrey *and* **Brooke**

Each of you is beautiful and special in your own way.
May you soar high and far, seek your best self according
to your unique design, and live with
theme and flame.

Table of Contents

Foreword   xi
Acknowledgments   xv
Introduction   xvii
Prologue   xix

1. **A New Beginning**   1
    Time to Celebrate!   1
    A Rude Awakening   3
2. **The One and Only You**   7
    A Joyful Child Living as Her Unique Self   7
    Farewell to a Carefree Childhood   13
    Individuality Fades into Conformity   15
    A New Experience in Diversity   15
    My Inner Voice Speaks Again   16
3. **Looking Behind the Mirror**   19
    A Blurred Picture   19
    You Are Expressed Through Your Unique Traits   21
    My Top Three Questions   22
        What Should I Do in Life?   22
        How Can I Live a Healthy Life?   25
        How Do I Transform My Personal Style?   26
    Get Deep into Your True Self   27
        Reflect on Your Life Experiences   28
        Get an Objective View of Yourself   28
        Build Vocabulary to Describe Yourself   31
    Accept Yourself, Completely   32
    Drive Self-transformation with Self-honesty   34
4. **Your Temperament is Permanent**   37
    Discover Your Temperament Type   38
    Connect the Dots into Patterns   40
    Reignite the Sparkles in Your Dreams   42
    Temperament in Organizations   43
    Overcome Cultural Bias   44
    Caveats to Watch For   47

5. **Your Priceless Natural Talents** 49
Your Talents May Not Appear Spectacular 51
How Natural Talents Impact Performance 51
Discover Your Natural Talents 53
Choose Professional Testing for Your Purpose 56
Live Like a Bird Flying with the Wind 58
What If "I Don't Have Much Talent?" 60
Mega Talent: Talent of Leveraging Talents 62
Enjoy the Best of Your Times 64
6. **Finding Passion in Your Purpose** 69
Interests Can Be Capricious 69
Be Careful with "Bogus Interests" 71
Passion: The Most Intense Interest 72
Dust Off Your Childhood 75
Most Telling Predictor of Greatness 77
Vanessa: A Life Driven by Passion 78
Which Path Will Your Passion Follow? 81
Ingredient for a Wonderful Life 82
7. **Values: The Guiding Lights** 85
Discover Your Values 86
Follow What's Truly Important to You 88
Unlearn Old Values and Embrace New Values 89
Work Is Unpleasant or Is It? 89
Job Security or Freedom of Choice? 91
Real Value of Money 94
Wisdom Behind Blessings 97
8. **Taking the Road Less Travelled** 101
The Future "Career" 103
Stay True to Core Beliefs 105
Risk Being a Fool in the Eyes of Others 106
Opportunities Are Often in Plain Sight 108
The Barrier of Loss Aversion 110
Yuriy and Inna: Taking the Road Less Travelled 111
The Fork in the Road 113
Compelled, Not Just Determined 114
"Is This It for Me?" 115

9. **Children Have Their Own Destinies**   119
    Children May Have Different Talents   120
    Respect but Guide Their Interests   122
    Seek Fulfillment Through Ourselves,
    Not Our Children   124
    Establish Healthy Self-esteem in Our Children   125
10. **What Is Your Health Philosophy?**   127
    Health Definition Leads to Health Destination   128
    Your Mind Influences Your Body   129
    Wisdom from My Father: Overcome Nature
    with Nurture   135
    Healthy Lifestyles Can Be Enjoyable   139
    Your Health Needs to Be "Your Way"   141
11. **Ideal Diet: The Diet That Is Right for You**   143
    Develop Your Personalized Diet Plan   144
    Be in Tune with Your Own Body   148
    Focus on the Quality of Foods   149
12. **Nutritional Supplementation: When Food
    Is Not Enough**   153
    Again, Quality Is the Key   156
    Your Personalized Supplementation Program   158
    My Health Transformation   160
13. **Your Exercise, Your Day**   163
    Tailor Your Exercise Program to Fit Yourself   164
    The Myths About Exercise   167
    Follow Your Biological Clock   168
    Take Charge of Your Health, Beginning Today   170
14. **Projecting Your Unique Style**   173
    The Years of Style Mishaps   173
    Style Is More Than a Fashion Statement   175
    My Style Transformation Begins   177
        Body Shape: Find Balance and Proportion   178
        Colors: What is Your Season?   180
        Face Shape: More Potential Than You Think   181
        Personality Also Plays a Role   182
    A New Way of Wardrobe Planning   182
    We Are All Beautiful, in Our Unique Ways   184

15. **Becoming Your Best Self**   185
   Being Unique Is Not "Appearing" Different   185
   More than "Just Being Myself"   186
   Develop Authentic Self-esteem   187
   Cultivate an Abundance Mindset   190
   Great Faith in Great Vision   192
   Move from "Can Not" to "Why Not"   194
   Overcome Fear of Judgment and Rejection   198
   Persevere in Your Actions   200
16. **Living with Theme and Flame**   203

Epilogue   211
References   213
About the Author   219

Foreword

I first met the author, Lydia Wei, more than two years ago at a business conference. A group of us were having breakfast together discussing some of our professional and personal goals for the near future. During the conversation, Lydia briefly shared her ongoing self-discovery journey, conducted over a period of several years.

It was a stimulating conversation. I noticed that her approach to learning about her own natural predispositions was much more detailed and refined than most of the general discussions in which I had been engaged before. Vibrant, insightful and inspiring, she is in her prime—with two daughters—yet still approaching life with childlike curiosity. Like an investigative reporter, she had taken it upon herself to go deep "behind the mirror" and reflected on her own life and lifestyle based on scientifically-validated studies.

She smiled, as we left the breakfast table, and said that maybe she should write a book about her self-discovery, in order to help more people realize their potential. I saw merit in her idea and encouraged her to go for it. With that said, I'll admit that I have heard hundreds of individuals tell me they were "thinking about writing a book." So, I smiled, shook hands and went about my own routine of lecturing and writing about high performance human behavior.

One day, surprisingly, I received an email from Lydia, reminding me of our brief meeting, and asking me—if it would not be an imposition— to review her manuscript and perhaps comment on its content and structure. Although I have received many drafts from aspiring authors in the past, I have made it a policy not to look over new ones because my schedule does not give me the opportunity to do justice to the author who has labored so intensely on his or her book. But I was so impressed that Lydia had actually followed through on her goal, that I agreed. Actually, I also was curious to learn about the research project she had undertaken so meticulously.

As she was finalizing the manuscript, I volunteered to offer a foreword. *"The Girl in the Chrysalis"* is completely different from any self-help book I have studied. Rather than a "rags to riches" autobiography, extolling the successes in her own life, Lydia Wei has focused on YOU, the reader, and what actions you can take to discover your own unique self.

Humble and vulnerable, she describes her transition from a free-spirited child into a highly regimented environment, in which her individuality faded into conformity. She then covers a journey of how she made the transition, two decades later, from someone living in conformity back into a free-spirited, unique woman.

As the chapters unfold, you will learn how to discover and pursue your true calling, by gaining knowledge of your unique temperament, natural talents, passions and values. You will also learn how differentiation and personalization can give you a competitive advantage in today's technology-driven world. Later in the book, she goes into depth in ways to develop and apply your personal health philosophy and healthy lifestyle—based upon your individual physical characteristics. Finally, you will gain insights on how to present yourself to the outside world, confidently and comfortably, with a personal style that expresses your unique physical features and personality.

Make no mistake, this is not your typical "feel good" book filled with popular clichés and celebrity-oriented anecdotes. You will want to read this book more than once and use a highlight marker to underline those suggestions she offers on time-tested, reputable research techniques utilized in authentic self-reflection and self-realization.

I believe that, through self-reflection, research and action, this gem of a book offers a fresh perspective on how to discover your true self and break free from those invisible, time-grown, cocoon-like limitations we all face. It will help you fly higher, farther and live a life with more purpose and passion, which Lydia describes as living by your unique design, with "theme and flame."

Denis Waitley, author

The Psychology of Winning
   &
Seeds of Greatness

Acknowledgments

First and foremost, I want to thank Dr. Denis Waitley for mentoring me on this book. Without your encouragement, the book wouldn't have been written. Without your guidance, the book would have been an assembly of scattered ideas.

I want to thank Chaz DeSimone for your wonderful cover design, and for your valuable input on the publishing process. Also appreciation to Dan Chen for portraying me in the best light and to Lisa Salan for your beautiful butterfly watercolors for the cover.

I want to thank each and every one of my friends, partners, and colleagues, for helping me, influencing me and shaping my life in your unique ways. Although I can't mention all of your names and stories in the book, you know who you are.

In particular, I want to thank those of you who have given me the privilege of sharing your stories, in the order of appearing in the book: Nahid Motahar, Linda Harris, Harold Harris, Vanessa Liao, Tao Tong, Laurie Guest, Yuriy Yurchuk, Inna Kostukovsky, Galina Kostukovsky, Lilian Tan, Frits Tan, Lilian Goldenberg, and Kathleen Ramey.

I want to thank you, mom and dad, for always being there for me; my brother, for being my biggest cheerleader from childhood through adulthood.

Last but not least, I want to thank you, my husband Weiying, for always supporting me in all of my endeavors, even if they seemed impractical at the time; my precious daughters, Audrey and Brooke, for supporting me in the best way you can—by being caring, responsible, independent children and by being understanding when I worked during many weekends. I wouldn't have been able to write the book without your patience, care and love. My life wouldn't have been complete without you.

Introduction

Although this is a story about my journey into self-discovery and self-transformation, my purpose is for it to shed light and meaning to you toward your own, unique trans-formation. These words are meant to express ideas, experiences and observations that may help you find your way to joy and fulfillment. Each of us needs to identify and break out of those cocoon-like chambers that we ourselves spin, unconsciously, preventing our transformation into our unique self.

I have included some of the detailed research and studies that I have undertaken in an effort to give you assurance that—in addition to learning from the trials and errors in life, which could be costly—it's possible to gain a deep insight of ourselves and fly free from our limiting, invisible barriers in more proactive and effective ways. I hope you, too, will discover who you are and live a life by your design, with theme and flame.

Prologue

The little girl looked forward, with enthusiasm, to her visits to the playground, right by her home in China. The playground was lined with tall, majestic Chinese white poplar trees. There was a gently flowing river nearby with mature willow trees on the banks swaying gracefully in the warm, summer breeze. These special moments would be etched, indelibly, in her mind and heart throughout her early and adult life; much more vivid and inspiring than any photos her family may have taken and saved in an album as reflections of those carefree, early years.

During one memorable outing, the little girl noticed something unusual hanging delicately from the branch of a tree. She had never seen anything like it before. What was this? At first glance, it appeared to be a twig, with a dried pod, like a pea-pod, attached to it. Standing on her tip-toes, she examined it more carefully, making sure not to touch it with her fingers. She thought she could see something inside the pod, but she could not tell what it was. Could this be some kind of flower ready to bloom? Who put it there? It almost looked as if there was a folded wing inside, with a pretty pattern on it. Was it alive? It seemed to be asleep or waiting.

Her parents smiled as she pointed excitedly and asked if they could explain what she saw. She learned that afternoon, so many years ago, that she had been introduced to her first chrysalis, the incubation chamber in which a caterpillar goes through the magical metamorphosis of becoming a lovely butterfly. This transformation is one of the most incredible processes among all living creations. It defies all logic that a mere caterpillar, like millions upon millions of other caterpillars, can completely change its form and destiny from an earthbound crawler into an exquisite, beautiful, soaring butterfly.

Even as the little girl marveled at this newly discovered phenomenon, she was not aware, at the time, that her own future could be compared to a series of similar transformations—transformations requiring her to break out of cocoon-like structures, created by both her early environment and her personal choices in life. She was, in reality, "The Girl in the Chrysalis."

A New Beginning

Not until we are lost do we begin to understand ourselves.
— *Henry David Thoreau*

December 11, 2009 was a memorable day for me. After four years in the MBA program, I graduated with honors from the University of Chicago Booth School of Business. It was one of the best educational experiences in my life. Our professors were top notch; our classmates were talented and motivated; and our classes were fun and exhilarating. I cherished every minute of it.

Time to Celebrate!

The graduation ceremony was held at the beautiful Rockefeller Memorial Chapel on the Hyde Park campus. It was a typical chilly and cloudy Chicago winter day, but the air was filled with warmth and excitement. I was surrounded by friends and family, including my parents, my husband, and my two lovely daughters, 5-year old Audrey and 2-year old Brooke. There was an enthusiastic buzz of conversations all around as congratulations were being exchanged.

As we lined up outside the chapel to get ready for the procession, I finally had some alone time. Many scenes from the past few years flew through my mind. These were no doubt the busiest years in my life, juggling priorities between school, homework, children and a regular job. But there were a lot of fond memories too.

It always made me smile when I thought of how my mom described my trip to the school to my aunt, "It's a journey for her to go to school. She needs to take three ways of transportation: car, train, and boat." It sounds really challenging, doesn't it?

I lived in the northern suburb of Chicago. It took me about an hour and a half to get to school. After work, I drove from my office to the nearby train station, hopped on the train, and got off at Chicago's Union Station. I then took the Chicago River water taxi, weather permitting, to Michigan Avenue and finally arrived at Gleacher Center, Booth's downtown campus. As my mom said, it was quite a journey.

The years in school also progressed in parallel with some of the most significant events in my family life. We moved from Houston to Chicago in March of 2005, one month after my first daughter, Audrey, was born. One day it occurred to me that the result of my GMAT test, taken several years ago, was going to expire. I realized that right here, locally, the University of Chicago offers one of the best MBA programs in the country. I submitted my application right away and began the evening/weekend program in September of 2005.

My second daughter Brooke was born in March of 2008, in the middle of my MBA program. Brooke was a tiny baby at birth. During the first two months, she always fell asleep during feeding; I literally needed to feed her every two hours. It was an exhausting 24-hour ordeal. Thankfully, she grew to be a healthy and strong baby in six months and I was able to go back to school and finish the program.

It was a big commitment to go to classes two nights a week with two little children at home. When I arrived home around eleven at night, they were already asleep. I would sit by them for a long time, just to watch them sleep, kiss their cute little faces, touch their chubby little feet, and feel so much tender love for them. I was deeply grateful that my husband and our parents took good care of them during those busy years.

As I replayed these scenes in my mind, I found myself approaching the podium. When I received my diploma, I saw Audrey and Brooke sitting in the audience, with big smiles and excitement on their faces. At that moment, it felt like all the work had been worth it. I was so glad to be their role model, and be someone they could be proud of. As we walked out of the Rockefeller Memorial Chapel, I felt happy and content.

A Rude Awakening

After the ceremony, we had a great time at the reception, meeting and talking with my friends. However, as we started to talk about our post-graduation plans, I felt a little embarrassed because I didn't have a plan—other than staying with the same corporate job. Most graduates had a well-designed plan, looking forward to exciting careers such as investment banking, asset management, and management consulting.

As a mom with two young children, I knew these popular careers, usually with long working hours or heavy travel, were not feasible for me. Deep inside, I also was not passionate about these particular careers. Honestly, I was not sure what I was passionate about, although I had always enjoyed subjects related to social science and humanities. That was why I had pursued concentrations in Economics and Management & Organizational Behavior. However, I had no idea how I could make the best use of them.

Suddenly, I felt a sense of emptiness. It was the end of an era, but what was the new beginning?

The sky already was dark as we left the Hyde Park campus. As we drove through the narrow streets of South Chicago, Christmas lights were twinkling along the streets and in the homes. It was a beautiful winter night, and we would be celebrating Christmas soon. I had every reason to feel a sense of pride and achievement, but I felt sad and somewhat unsettled. The children were tired from all the excitement and quickly fell asleep. As I watched their innocent faces, I was no longer sure if I was on the right path to be a role model for them and to guide them toward a fulfilling life.

In spite of everything I had accomplished, I had never felt truly fulfilled. Everything was perfect on the surface, but beneath the surface, I lived a mediocre life. I chased the goals thrown to me by my circumstances and the dreams that were often "other people's dreams." I easily got lost in choices and temptations, and was tossed and blown about by every wind of change.

When I faced major decisions in life, I looked outside to see what was popular in the moment. Unfortunately, what was popular in the moment kept changing. I ended up like a rudderless ship trying to reach some vague port of call in a vast, unfriendly sea, sailing in many directions without a compass. The ship sailing in many directions is essentially sailing without direction, and a ship without direction is always navigating against the wind.

If there was anything for which I could give myself credit, it was that I tried to apply to my future decisions what I had learned from my trial and error lessons. Although Booth has a legendary finance program, I resisted the temptation to enroll in some of the most popular finance courses. I was determined to take only the courses in which I was genuinely interested.

For the first time in my adult life, I felt that I was deliberately making choices that were not the most popular.

I was somewhat nervous and unsure, but deep inside I knew it was the right direction, which turned out to be true years later. This was the first expression of my desire to regain individuality.

As I reflected on my life experiences, I felt a strong desire to get in touch with my true self. I had to answer some big questions before rushing into the next good thing: Who am I? How can I live a fulfilling life? How can I guide my children to live joyful and meaningful lives?

Armed with a determination to find my true self, I embarked on a journey of self-discovery and self-transformation. As I have learned, this is a lifelong journey which would evolve continuously as I grow. Today, I am not at the destination yet, but I am well on the path to live as I am designed. I live a joyful and fulfilling life, with clarity and purpose. I still have much to learn, but I feel that I have wind beneath my wings.

2

The One and Only You

> You are the only you God made...
> God made you and broke the mold.
> —*Max Lucado*

Although I lost touch with my inner self as I grew up, I enjoyed a wonderful childhood which allowed me to fully express myself. The idea of individual uniqueness was too deep for a child's mind to process, but intuitively I knew I was special, just as my young friends were special in their own, individual ways. I also knew how it felt to live freely, just as I was.

A Joyful Child Living as Her Unique Self

I was born in a small village in Tianjin, China. Both of my parents were teachers. My mom was a teacher at the local middle school. My dad used to be a teacher at the same middle school, but later he served as the principal of the local night school, a special type of school helping the illiterate villagers learn how to read and write.

The middle school was composed of two rows of one-story buildings. The front row functioned as classrooms and the back row served as teachers' offices and teachers' homes, which was where we lived. There was a playground in front of the classrooms, lined by tall Chinese white poplar trees. At the other end of the playground was a river, with old willow trees swaying by the river banks and river weeds flowing in the clear water. The smell of summer was heavenly there, an earthy mix of the sun-kissed vegetation, the white poplars, the willows, and the river weeds.

The middle school and the villages nearby were the settings of my most precious childhood memories. I was high spirited and somewhat daring as a child. When I was four years old, I was already running all over the place with my friends. We loved to spend time on the playground, by the river, and in the farm lands where there were fields of wheat, corn, vegetables, and watermelons. When we were thirsty or hungry, we would stop by a nearby villager's house to get water and food. Everyone in our village knew each other.

Every time I saw the African proverb posted in my daughter's school lobby, "It takes a village to raise a child," I thought of my own childhood. This was not just a slogan to me, but a reality I lived.

Both my parents were well known and well respected in the area they served. They loved and cared for their students as if each of them was one of their own children. At that time, many villagers didn't understand the value of education. They would prefer that their children help with the farm work, rather than attend school. Although it was beyond their academic duties, my parents spent many nights visiting these families and persuading the parents to keep their children in school.

As there were no other methods of transportation, they often walked more than an hour just to get to the students' homes. Additionally, they volunteered many Sundays, the only days off back then, to help students with their school work. They literally changed the courses of life for many of their students, who come to visit them and thank them even today, many decades later.

Every season, to express gratitude to my parents, the villagers would share with us the fresh produce they grew. Our food was truly 100% organic and natural at that time. I especially loved the freshly picked fruits and vegetables in summer. One day, someone dropped a few big winter melons at our door. I was home alone and thought it would be nice to help my parents prepare one for dinner.

I managed to roll one winter melon into the house, and tried to cut it apart with a kitchen knife. The winter melon was not easy to maneuver as it had a round and smooth surface. The knife cut into my finger soon after I started. The cut was so deep that I thought I would lose my finger. I cried and screamed as I ran to my mom's classroom. All the students stuck their heads out of the classroom window to see what catastrophe had happened.

Although I got scolded badly, I begged my parents to cook the winter melon for dinner. It was one of the most delicious dinners I can remember.

My brother was born when I was five. He was a cute baby with bright, twinkling eyes. He was a lot of fun and his antics were a constant source of entertainment and laughter.

The best part of my brother's day was when he picked up the eggs that the hens had laid. As a toddler, he loved animals and took good care of the chickens. His face glowed with pride whenever he handed the eggs to us, as if he had waved a magic wand to make them appear in the basket.

The best part of my day was the morning routine with my dad. Every morning we walked hand in hand to a small shop to get freshly made soybean milk and tofu. We talked to everyone we met along the way. I enjoyed listening to adults discussing the happenings in the village. This daily experience set the stage for my future interest in verbal interactions and curiosity about different cultural beliefs.

My parents earned a meager salary. Although we lived with bare minimum material possessions, I never felt lacking. In fact, I felt very rich because I had everything I needed as a child, including food, shelter, nature, and friends. More importantly, I had abundant freedom, security and love.

Although my parents taught me many safety rules, I broke the rules often and created many frustrating and anxious moments for them. One day, I was still not home by late night. My parents searched everywhere in the village nearby. Although they didn't believe I would go that far, my dad went on to search in a village farther away. The closest path to that village ran across a graveyard. It was pitch black as there was no night lighting in the villages. The trees rustled loudly in the wind. This surely could be described as one of the scariest scenes in our culture.

After a while, my dad noticed an apparition of a small object moving through the tombstones in the distance. Although he was never superstitious, he couldn't help thinking, that night, about the real possibility of the existence of living ghosts. He cautiously kept moving forward until he recognized me as that small, glimmering apparition, greeting him in a cheerful and fearless mood, as if we had merely been playing a game of hide and seek.

When winter came, I liked to play on sleds with my friends on the frozen lake, without my parents' knowledge or approval. One day as I slid very close to the shore, the ice started to crack. Before I knew it, my legs fell through the ice into the frigid water. I held on to the sled desperately trying to keep my chest and head above the water.

My friends on the shore yelled and ran to find tree branches long enough to reach where I struggled in the water. They managed to pull me to safety. I will always remember the combination of horror and relief on my parents' faces when I showed up shivering, chilled and soaking wet at our front door. In spite of these incidents, after which they disciplined me, my parents gave me the space and freedom to express my personality, and they accepted and loved me.

The only reason I am sharing these very personal experiences which are, perhaps, only meaningful to me and my own life, is that I am hoping they will strike a half-forgotten chord in your own memory bank, connecting your present life to your early childhood. As we will discuss later in the book, an integral piece in the puzzle of self-discovery is to dust off your childhood memories and recall what brought you the most passion, enjoyment and impact.

My childhood experiences had a profound impact on my life. To a great extent, I attribute my inner confidence and security to my bountifully free and joyful childhood. Growing up, I always had a smile on my face when I conversed. Those early events also implanted the courage in me to continuously explore new challenges and pursue my dreams in life. I am deeply grateful to my parents for giving me the freedom to explore the world, as a child and as an adult, in spite of the risks and mistakes involved.

I admit that, like many parents today, sometimes I am overly protective with my own children. Of course, our children face a very different environment and culture today. Still, from time to time, I need to remind myself to relax and live in faith.

Like ourselves, our children will experience risks and challenges in life, which we can't always control as parents. We need to give them knowledge and wisdom to handle the situations that may arise, and then we have to relax and pray that our children will be protected by grace and by our example.

As a child, I flourished like the seedling of a tree growing in fertile soil. Everything happened naturally at its own appointed time. When I was six years old, I became curious about school. On a hot summer day, I walked to the local elementary school by myself. The classroom doors were open to allow fresh air in. I stood by the door of a classroom, quietly listening, and stuck my head in and out trying not to be noticed.

The teacher was reading, and writing words on the blackboard as she read. She noticed me and walked out to talk to me. She must have seen me before, because she asked if I was the child of my parents. Then she asked if I wanted to join the class. I was thrilled and, of course, answered, "Oh yes, I would!" I happily sat through the class for the whole day. This was how I started school.

Although I was not of school age, my parents and the teacher thought if I loved the school so much, they could just add an extra desk and see how I responded. To me, the classroom was like a candy store. I was hungry with curiosity and desire to learn.

Because I did well in exams, I was able to move up grades with my classmates. When the elementary school system was changed from a total of five years to six years, I jumped another grade, and remained as the youngest child through my college years.

In many ways, the elementary school was like an extended family for me. My classmates took care of me as a younger sister. We loved to play long rope jumping. Two friends swung the rope while the other four or five friends took turns jumping. If someone tripped while jumping, she would need to return to the unexciting task of swinging the rope. I was the only one allowed to jump as much as I wanted without having to swing the rope.

I learned that being young and small could be just as great as being older and taller. I also relished the warm feeling of being in the company of a loving support group, which is not always the environment experienced by young children, especially today.

As a child, I constantly experienced what psychologists called "flow," a mental state characterized by energized focus, complete absorption and deep enjoyment in the activity performed. This feeling was planted deeply in my heart, and many years later, it would be rekindled at significant turning points in my life—turning points in the lifelong transformation of the girl in the chrysalis into a woman seeking to fly freely toward a destiny of theme and flame.

Farewell to a Carefree Childhood

Toward the end of my elementary school years, my parents decided to move from the village I had always called home to a nearby town, in order to facilitate the best possible education for myself and my brother. The town had the best elementary school, middle school, and high school in the area. The move opened a new chapter in my life. I experienced some real challenges for the first time in my life.

My parents made a lot of sacrifices during this move. We didn't own personal real estate property back then. Government employee's housing was allocated by the government and through the employee's work place. Because housing was not readily available in my parents' new work place, we didn't have a home for two years. The four of us were scattered in four separate locations. My brother lived with my grandma. I lived with my mom's aunt. My mom and my dad lived in each of their respective offices.

This abrupt uprooting of our family unit caused some emotionally trying times, especially when the four of us were reunited for a short visit, and then I had to say a tearful goodbye again. This unsettling lifestyle was aggravated by the fact that my parents had to leave the students they loved, and the villagers they had befriended for so many years. It was as if we were beginning our lives all over again in a strange, unfamiliar environment. Although I was sad about the changes, I understood the sacrifices my parents had made for us and I was committed to do my best to honor them.

The move also marked the end of a childhood filled with freedom and joy. As I entered middle school, I became part of a regimented and highly competitive educational system, in which students were evaluated solely based on test results. We shared a common mission, which was to study hard, get high scores and then enter a good college. Much has been said concerning the shortcomings of China's strict, cookie-cutter education system. In recent years, this criticism has become increasingly harsh as Chinese citizens have learned more about the western education system.

To me, there are always two sides of the same coin. In spite of its drawbacks, the education system my brother and I experienced was fair and efficient given the unique socioeconomic conditions in China. To its credit, it offered a solid academic foundation, and instilled valuable life management qualities such as discipline, focus and perseverance. These qualities have served me well in all my pursuits as I have grown from childhood into adulthood.

There is no doubt that our move to the larger, more populated town was one of the best decisions my parents made as they considered the future for my brother and me. My brother and I later entered two of the top universities in China. Without my parents' difficult choice, we were unlikely to have had the type of education and pursued the opportunities and goals available to us today. Had my parents sought to maintain the more secure status quo in our quiet village life, the journey toward my own self-actualization may never have begun or even been considered.

Because I am keenly aware of the tradeoffs involved in virtually every decision in life, I always look at the bright side in life and dwell on the desired outcome in any situations. I endeavor to focus on the present and the future, and reflect on rather than regret past events. In this book, you will read about a few poor decisions I made in the past, but even these decisions offered important learning and served as stepping stones for future success.

Everything has its timing and offers benefits along with limitations. Although I lost touch with my individuality after middle school, I developed in many positive ways during those formative years, for which I am forever grateful.

Individuality Fades into Conformity

As time passed after middle school, I no longer felt that unique, high spirited child within me. My individuality faded into conformity. Because I was no longer able to define myself in intrinsic terms, I learned to define myself by external factors, such as what I do, what I have, and particularly, to which group I belong.

Within each of the groups to which I belonged, we tended to live similar lifestyles, and even had similar dress codes and fashion tastes. I remember that one year in college, white scarves were suddenly in fashion. Before long, everyone on the streets was wearing a white scarf. During this period, the notion that "each individual is unique" never entered my mind.

Of course, we all recognized that some people were special. Some people had special status, such as royal families. Some people had special achievements, such as renowned scientists. Some people had special talents, such as artists, musicians and athletes. But these special people only accounted for a very small percentage of the population. I, certainly, was not one of them.

A New Experience in Diversity

In 1998, I came to the United States. My eyes were opened to diversity and individuality. It was fascinating to meet people from different cultures, with different looks, interests and lifestyles.

Nahid, my immigration attorney, was one of the people I found to be very different and special. Nahid moved to the

U.S. from Iran. She was an accomplished attorney and a woman deeply rooted in her faith. For two and a half years, she took time out of her law practice and lived in Haifa, Israel to provide volunteer service.

She was elegant, intelligent and independent; yet humble, kind, with great hospitality. She had a beautiful home decorated with exquisite Persian carpets and artifacts. She invited my husband and me over whenever she held parties in her home. Through these occasions, she introduced us to many aspects of Persian culture, including some of the delicious and exotic cuisine, such as Persian saffron rice.

In many ways, Nahid inspired my interest in different cultures and appreciation for different cultures. I was fascinated that every culture could be so different yet so uniquely beautiful. It was the same way with every individual, as I later learned. I also saw through her that women, regardless of cultural background, could live a successful, beautiful and multidimensional life. I have fond memories of her even after many years have passed.

Although I met Nahid and many other different and special people, I didn't see myself special in any way. I considered myself as one of the most ordinary people living the most ordinary life. I guess this is how a majority of the individuals view themselves.

My Inner Voice Speaks Again

In 2003, a series of events led me to my faith. While I could comprehend that God loves the world, it was difficult to grasp that God cares for me and has a plan for me as a unique individual. For a long time, I struggled with the question, how could God know me and love me out of the seven billion people in the world? The enlightenment began when I accidentally came across a few articles on how biometrics identifications impacted security technologies.

We have known for a long time that no two people on earth have the same finger prints. Today, scientists are discovering more and more biometrics that are unique at the individual level. We are unique in our footprints, even in our lip prints! There are subtle differences in each of us in innate characteristics such as ear shape, iris pattern, and the pattern of retina blood vessels. We also are different from one another in the shape of our veins in the palms of our hands, the sound frequencies at which we speak, and the electrical signals of our heart activities.

I began to understand that on a biological level, each of us is indeed created in a unique and special way. I already was feeling a profound spiritual awareness as I marveled at the beauty of life itself. As a mother, I had been continually amazed that I was granted the privilege of bringing two daughters into this world; they were both so special and yet so different from each other.

Realizing that each human being is uniquely made, out of the seven billion people who live on earth today, and out of the hundreds of billions of people who ever lived and will live on earth, was and continues to be an overwhelming experience. The incredible wisdom and love behind the creation of life have been both inspiring and humbling.

Thinking back to that day when, as a little girl, I noticed a chrysalis on a tree branch, it was so exciting to stare at that pod with the butterfly inside, undergoing such a dramatic transformation. My parents told me that butterflies are nourished by the nectar in flowers and that they pollinate many different species of flowers.

Recently, I learned that there are about 20,000 types of butterflies and over 400,000 kinds of flowers in the world. Each of the flowers has a distinctly different design, aroma and thrives in a different environment, but each of the flowers is perfect in its own uniqueness.

Like the flower, each of us is perfect in our own uniqueness. Some people have black eyes; some people have blue eyes. Some people are introverts; some people are extroverts. Some people are good at art; some people are good at science. As the Yoga master Prem Prakash said, "Each soul has its own note to sing in the divine chorus and no voice is more important than another." Our journey is to discover our note to sing and let our voice be heard.

3

Looking Behind the Mirror

He who knows others is wise;
he who knows himself is enlightened.
—*Lao Tzu*

Spiritually, I was able to comprehend that God created each individual with a unique plan. Scientifically, I was able to confirm that each individual was created uniquely based on biometric discoveries. Practically, however, these conceptual understandings didn't make a major difference in my life until I acquired a concrete, specific understanding of how exactly I was unique, and then consciously developing and projecting my personal uniqueness throughout my life.

A Blurred Picture

When I began the self-discovery process, I was unable to grasp my uniqueness in a personal and meaningful way. I didn't have the special talents, special achievements, special interests, special background...that I usually associated with special people. As much as I wanted to believe I was unique, all I could see in myself was a blurred, plain vanilla kind of face that you would meet every day on the streets.

I reflected on a series of questions such as, how I was different from the people around me, what I enjoyed most and least, and what I was good at and poor at. I had some vague ideas, but was unable to articulate them. After a period of frustrations, I realized that I was not going to see the forest by staying in the forest. I needed to get out of the forest, climb aboard a virtual helicopter, and view the forest from a new, elevated vantage point.

I dove into reading and research to get new perspectives and insights. It opened up a fascinating world for me. My self-discovery, and self-transformation in parallel, have since turned into a lifelong journey and a passion that has only deepened with time. During the journey, I learned how I was unique as an individual, and how I could apply this self-knowledge to transform my life and live with joy and fulfillment.

My stories are meant to inspire you to find your uniqueness, in your unique ways. People have different learning styles and approaches to life. I am more of a read/write learner, and my husband is more of a kinetics learner. When we bought a new camera, I would not touch it until I read the manual. But my husband would immediately jump in to explore it. He wouldn't touch the manual unless he encountered questions or problems.

Similarly, it may work best for some of you, like me, to go through a methodical self-discovery process, and systematically apply the knowledge to design your life. It may work best for others of you to engage in a variety of activities, and figure out who you are based on hands-on experiences. I heard about a man who was a successful entrepreneur in the investment field. In his early years, he had worked in many different fields such as a tour guide, a translator and a nightclub singer, before he concluded that he was destined to be a professional investor.

No matter what your learning style and approach to life are, you may find value in my journey as you set out to discover your unique self. Throughout the journey, the most significant takeaway I want to share with you is that, "know thyself" is the ultimate enlightenment, as both ancient Chinese and Greeks recognized. The more self-knowledge you have, the more power you have to live a truly fulfilling life. While recognizing our limitations, the key to fulfillment is to concentrate on our unique strengths. This will take us as far and as high as we dare to dream.

You Are Expressed Through Your Unique Traits

Our individual uniqueness is expressed through our inborn traits and acquired traits. The inborn traits, such as temperament, natural talents, and physiological design, are embedded in our DNA at the moment of our conception. They are comprised of all the seeds, the biological templates and the raw materials, given to us at birth. These traits are inborn, innate, inherent, and demonstrate themselves consistently throughout our lifetime. This is why we say that they are "in our nature."

The acquired traits are the types of traits that are shaped by our environment and our choices, such as our mindset, attitudes, values, interests, passions, skills and certain aspects of our personalities. This is why we say that they are "in our nurture."

Scientists continue to debate which influence is more important: heredity or environment. Evidence supports both positions. Identical twins tend to have similar personality traits whether they are raised together or apart. This indicates that we inherit many of our personality traits from our parents. Yet adopted children also tend to share traits with their adoptive parents. This suggests the opposite conclusion: the environment we grow up in has a decisive effect on our behavior. In short, heredity and environment both have an important impact on our behavior.

In reality, our inborn traits and acquired traits are intertwined. They work hand in hand to determine who we are and how our lives will be shaped. Although some scientists believe that our inborn traits dominate our destinies, there is increasing evidence that acquired traits are critical, as they can be reshaped, redirected and reordered to produce a life filled with joy, productivity and significance, regardless of the genetic cards that we were dealt at conception.

Inborn traits can point to the direction a person is best suited to pursue, but acquired traits often determine the specific path a person chooses and how far he or she can go along that path. It's not uncommon to see people with great talents accomplish little in life, while people with moderate talents accomplish a great deal. Our mindset, attitudes and values can make a huge difference in terms of the degree to which we can grow and achieve our potential.

My Top Three Questions

We can engage in self-discovery to learn about our uniqueness in various dimensions. The specific dimensions to focus on are determined by our purpose and goals. My self-discovery goals have evolved over time. When I started the journey, after the rude awakening around my MBA graduation, I primarily focused on answering three questions.

What Should I Do in Life?

At the time, I felt that I was living a life of mediocrity, without a clear direction and a sense of genuine fulfillment. I also recognized a lack of coherence and focus in my activities. Although I was always busy at something, the busy activities didn't get me very far.

During a recent cleanup of my home basement, I found a pile of the textbooks from eighteen years ago when I was engaged in studies for my master's degree in Information Systems. I flipped through the pages, and felt like I was reading something from ancient times—what I learned had long become obsolete.

As I reluctantly sent the books to the recycling bin—because they no longer had resale value—I couldn't help wondering how many years I had spent in blindly acquiring knowledge. In addition to the Master's Program in Information Systems, I also took scattered courses here and there on various other subjects.

I accepted, literally, the statement that "knowledge is power," reasoning that the more knowledge I accumulated, the more powerful I would become. With a huge price paid in tuition, time and energy, I acquired a large body of highly specialized knowledge that I had not used and would never use. It became obvious because this particular knowledge was a mismatch with my talents and interests, just as that expensive dress I owned was ill-fitting for my shape.

There is no question that a solid education is absolutely essential to succeed in life. I would not be where I am today without the education I have received. However, "knowledge is power" can be a misleading philosophy. Knowledge is power only when it can be applied and utilized for a worthwhile purpose. The knowledge that I acquired, but never used, had little power because it did not benefit me or society in a meaningful way.

When I was younger and free, I looked up to people who were engaged in many activities and constantly on the go. I only learned later, from my own experience, that being busy was not equal to being productive, was not equal to being successful, and was certainly not equal to being fulfilled in life.

In addition to its generic meaning of being busy, the word "busyness" has a second definition as "lively but meaningless activities." Unfortunately, for many of us, our busyness very often falls under the second definition.

The reality is, everyone has 24 hours a day. The busiest person on earth couldn't be busier than that. Given two people, with similar background and being busy for the same number of hours every day, why does one constantly grow and the other forever feel stuck? Why does one live with joy and the other live with dread? Why does one become a millionaire and the other struggle to make ends meet?

There are, of course, various reasons that could cause the differences. But one main reason, among many, is that people make different choices in life, and often, choices matter more than effort. There is a popular saying in China, "A bee is busy every day; everyone loves it. A mosquito is busy every day; everyone despises it. It's not how busy you are that is important, but what you are busy at."

I loved Simon Sinek's TED speech "Start with Why." In this speech, he emphasized that successful businesses start with a "why," then "what" and the very last, "how." The same goes with successful individuals. I, however, had approached life from the opposite direction. I was trapped in the doing without a clear "why" guiding it, like pulling a wagon without knowing the destination.

Some of you, like the old me, probably would say, "Of course, I have had a 'why' for everything I do!" Why do you stick to a job you are bored with? "I need to make a living." Why do you spend so much time watching TV? "I need to relax and entertain myself." Why do you not attend the business seminar with the best minds in your profession, if you want to build a better business and better future for your son? "I need to take my son to his swimming lesson. It's twenty dollars a lesson that I have paid!" These superficial answers do not represent the kind of "why" we are discussing here.

What we need is a big, overarching, compelling "why," rooted in who we are as a unique individual and what we truly want from life, much like the strategy for a business. This powerful "why" will enable us to look at things from a strategic, long term, proactive perspective instead of a tactical, short term, reactive perspective.

If we test everything we do, big or small, against this "why," it will give us fresh insight. For the mom above, if her "why" is really to build a better business and better future for her son, she could've rescheduled or canceled the swimming lesson and attended the business seminar. In the long run, she being a successful role model contributes more to her son's future than one swimming lesson, or, twenty dollars.

I was eager to find my own powerful "why" so that I could focus on the things that are truly essential, meaningful and fulfilling for the rest of my life.

How Can I Live a Healthy Life?

Nothing is more fundamental to a good life than health. However, as it is said, health is our greatest wealth but we never have a true idea of its value until we lose it. During the six years prior to my MBA graduation, I moved to Chicago, had two babies and went to school on top of working. The amount of mental and physical stress took a heavy toll on my health.

I began to experience chronic fatigue, low resistance to sickness and other symptoms of health deterioration. Every day when I got home after work, I was so exhausted that I had to rest for at least half an hour before I could function again. Surprisingly, all the numbers from my annual physical exam looked stellar. When the nurse saw my report, she even gasped and said, "Wow, congratulations! I haven't seen someone as healthy as you are for years!"

As I learned from the statistics, only 5% of the people in the world are truly healthy; 20% have various diseases; 75% are in a sub-health condition which is a gray state between health and disease. In this gray state, all the medical tests indicate normal readings, however, the person feels various discomforts such as chronic fatigue, feeling cold, low resistance to cold or flu, as it was in my case.

If disease represents the tip of an iceberg, the sub-health condition is that enormous lower portion of an iceberg, hidden deeply below the surface. To a certain extent, the invisible enemy is more challenging to handle than the visible one. Most people, even doctors, can't recognize it although the crises are silently brewing. The traditional medicine, for the most part, is not helpful in addressing the sub-health conditions.

At that point, I knew I must take ownership of my health. I also realized that general health advice didn't always apply to me. It is often tailored to address the common health risks, but not necessarily working the best for people in uncommon situations.

Although a low salt diet is considered healthier for most people, a diet slightly higher in salt could be beneficial to some people with low blood pressure. It's always wise to understand the rationale behind some general health advice and assumptions. Given my health situation, I felt the need to develop a personalized health approach.

How Do I Transform My Personal Style?

When I was a little child in China, my parents and teachers instilled in me that academic performance was all that counted and how we looked was not important. This was the belief of most parents and teachers at that time.

I was a bookworm child. It wasn't until I entered college that I started to care about my looks. Because my style education was nearly blank, I experienced many style mishaps as I grew up, which, to some extent, impacted my self-esteem. I developed the belief that I was not born to be stylish and beautiful. I could do nothing about it other than accepting it with peace.

Although I learned later in life that a good sense of style was important, the old belief had continued to hold me back until there came the moment of awakening during my maternity leave, after the birth of my second daughter Brooke.

I took a deep breath as Brooke finally fell asleep. In my precious break, I took a long look at myself in the mirror. I saw myself in the drab black and ivory colored maternity clothing, with a tired face, messy hair, and of course, the extra fifteen pounds. I was overwhelmed by sadness and self-pity. Although I had never thought I looked beautiful, this picture was strikingly worse.

In the midst of the sadness, I thought of my two beautiful girls, four-year old Audrey and baby Brooke. An inner voice came into my consciousness and whispered the questions: Do you want to be a role model to them with this kind of look? Do you want to teach them that looks are not important, while you know it is not true? Do you want to live with your style ignorance and simply say sorry, if they ever come to you for guidance?

As I contemplated these questions, I felt a fresh, intense wave of motivation to learn about style and to transform my sense of style, for myself and for my daughters. Although I didn't realize it at the time, it was the prelude to my full-fledged self-discovery.

In order to answer the three questions, I focused on the three inborn traits: temperament, natural talents and physical characteristics. I also clarified my core values and passions, which are acquired traits influenced by both my inborn traits and my life experiences.

Get Deep into Your True Self

My self-discovery involved asking thought-provoking questions to myself and to important people in my life, and reflecting on my internal feedback as well as the feedback from others. In addition, I researched relevant professional resources and took professional assessments.

Reflect on Your Life Experiences

Self-reflection is a key element in self-discovery. No one knows our life experiences, our deep thoughts and feelings better than ourselves. Self-discovery questions, such as "What were you recognized for as a child?" can provoke our thoughts and help us gain more clarity during self-reflection. A lot of self-discovery questions can be found online. You can ask the same questions to your family, your friends and other people with whom you feel comfortable. Their feedback will be very valuable too.

It's challenging to grasp our unique traits purely based on self-reflection and others' feedback. As we grow up, we become less in touch with our true self. Our thoughts and behaviors are more and more influenced by the environment and the people around us. On top of that, we often lack the ability to objectively evaluate ourselves, as well as the vocabulary to articulate our traits. Therefore, the next step I took was to explore professional resources and test options so that I could get a more objective view of myself and acquire the vocabulary to describe myself.

Get an Objective View of Yourself

It's difficult to objectively assess ourselves without some kinds of benchmarks or references. Taking aptitude as an example, in order to determine my most compelling aptitudes, there is an inherent comparison between how each aptitude is demonstrated in me and in others, and between how different aptitudes are demonstrated within myself. I may have some rough ideas from experiences, but the ideas may not be accurate without objective benchmarks.

People may overestimate an aptitude. In fact, it's a psychological finding that people tend to overestimate themselves, and as psychologist David Dunning said, "... more than that, they really seem to believe it." Research

28

conducted by David Dunning and another psychologist Justin Kruger has given the term "Dunning–Kruger effect"— a cognitive bias in which individuals suffer from illusory superiority, mistakenly assessing their ability as much higher than it really is.

Many surveys and social phenomena have testified the validity of this effect. One of the surveys was attached to the SAT exams. It asked the students to rate themselves relative to the median of the samples on a few positive characteristics. In ratings of leadership, 70% of the students put themselves above the median. In ratings of getting along well with others, 85% put themselves above the median and 25% rated themselves in the top 1%.

Some people, with an overestimate of their own abilities, erroneously believe that they are not successful in life because their abilities are not being recognized. Furthermore, they believe that others' successes are undeserved because those people, with lower abilities, must succeed through luck or cutting corners. These beliefs lead to frustrations and even bitterness.

The problem is that their "superior" abilities are often self-perceived. These abilities are neither confirmed by their performance nor validated based on objective benchmarks or honest feedback.

Being "lucky" or "unlucky" usually involves deep, underlying causes which are often unnoticed by those who are most frustrated. Even if we are able to objectively view ourselves, success often involves more than what we think.

After just graduating from college, still young and naïve, I thought I should be placed much higher on the corporate ladder because of my analytical ability. As I later learned, being a successful corporate executive involves much broader skills, such as leadership, communication, relationship building and sometimes, even the ability to create a perception of "executive presence."

Despite the fact that they have great abilities, many individuals still can't go far in life because of limitations imposed by their vision, mindset, attitudes and behaviors.

As I have learned in life, it is better to focus on desired outcomes and continuous improvement, rather than on being under-appreciated for my talents and abilities.

Although people often overestimate an aptitude, people also can underestimate an aptitude. Because an ability comes easily to them, they may think that it's the case for anyone. My friend never considered her manual dexterity as a talent until I pointed it out to her. It had always just seemed natural to her.

Sometimes people may not be aware of an aptitude. I was not aware of my music aptitude until I became engaged in singing lessons as an adult. Children today participate in many activities, but children of my generation grew up with very limited extracurricular activities. There were fewer opportunities to reveal some of our natural talents.

Of the natural talents that have been identified, nearly all of us have at least 3 to 5 of these innate aptitudes. Many individuals fail to discover these gifts until they are adults. They remain fully invested in careers they have pursued out of financial necessity, even if they are not passionate or particularly talented in these careers.

We can leverage professional tests to help discover or confirm where we really are. As a cautious tip about the tests, I personally would only invest in proven tests that are research-based and professionally developed by credible sources.

The tests online and in magazines are in abundance today, some of which are scientifically documented and most of which are simply based on current fads, more often entertaining than enlightening. When you look at a test, you want to consider the author and authentication, as it's difficult to evaluate the reliability of the testing methods and measurement standards.

Build Vocabulary to Describe Yourself

In addition to the challenge in lacking benchmarks, another challenge in self-discovery is in lacking the vocabulary to clearly and accurately describe our traits. To become an expert in any domain, we need master the vocabulary in that domain.

A wine connoisseur needs to master the vocabulary concerning wine; a football player needs to master the vocabulary specific to football; and a musician needs to master the vocabulary associated with music. In a similar way, people who want to understand their unique self need to master the vocabulary to describe their characteristics.

Words carry our thoughts and feelings. We can gain much more clarity about our thoughts and feelings when we have the words to properly describe them. A critical step in enhancing emotional intelligence is to develop the vocabulary that accurately describes emotions as they are being experienced. If you feel angry, can you further identify what kind of anger you feel? Is it irritation, frustration, contempt, bitterness, resentment, envy or jealousy? The more words you have to describe emotions, the more easily you are able to identify your emotions, understand the triggers behind your emotions, and sort out your emotions.

It works the same way when it comes to self-discovery. The more vocabulary we acquire about the different traits, the more precisely we can describe our unique characteristics, and the more deeply we can get to know who we are. We can acquire a large vocabulary in each area we explore— temperament, natural talents or other areas—through reading and researching professional resources available on the subject.

Research has proven that a large and rich vocabulary is directly related to success in our professional as well as personal lives. Most of our daily lives involve expressing our thoughts, feelings and ideas. Sometimes it is in a form of an inner dialog, where a rich and precise vocabulary facilitates clearer thinking and therefore leads to more effective actions. Sometimes it is in a form of dialog with others, where a good vocabulary facilitates communication with those who can be sounding boards and spring boards to help us become more successful.

Because vocabulary is so fundamental to the expression of all other natural aptitudes, it is measured as a separate aptitude in some professional aptitude tests. We can have many wonderful traits and talents inside of us, but without a large and precise vocabulary to express ourselves, we won't be able to take full advantage of these abilities. Another way to say this is that limited vocabulary and a lesser ability to communicate keeps many people with excellent abilities from developing and profiting from the abilities.

The good news is that, vocabulary can be improved with effort and discipline. Regardless of their level of education, most people use only about four hundred words in more than 80% of their everyday conversation, although there are over 450,000 words in an unabridged English dictionary. If we were to learn only ten new words each day for one year, we could become among the most learned and well-spoken individuals. Increased reading of both fiction and non-fiction works can be richly rewarding. In addition to building vocabulary, knowledge is gained, imagination is stimulated, and communication skills are enhanced.

Accept Yourself, Completely

Self-acceptance is the foundation for a truly meaningful self-discovery. As we grow up, we typically form certain views about what we like or dislike about ourselves. It's natural to view our unfavorable features in isolation, regarding each as a sign of individual weakness. In addition to unconscious self-denial, sometimes people consciously manipulate the answers in a test to avoid a result that they don't want to see, which defeats the purpose of self-discovery.

Initially, I didn't want to see what I disliked about myself as part of my uniqueness. After all, we all want to see ourselves as uniquely good, uniquely smart and uniquely competent. Who wants to look in the mirror and see themselves as unique in negative ways?

I held a negative view of myself for many years because of my ineptitude in sports. As a child, I tripped and fell often. The scars visible on my knees are still witness to that. As I grew up, I was typically one of the bottom students in the Physical Education class. During my college years, the sport facilities were very limited in China. Only the top students in Physical Education class could enroll in the interesting activities, such as tennis, swimming etc.

As the bottom students, I and another girl were placed in the boys' soccer class because there was no room for us in other activities. Basically, when the boys had their practices and games, the two of us just kicked a soccer ball in the corner of the field. I still recall my feelings of inadequacy and awkwardness as we kicked the soccer ball back and forth to each other. It was too embarrassing to treat this ineptitude as part of my uniqueness.

The positive news is, just as self-discovery demands self-acceptance, self-discovery also facilitates self-acceptance. My perspectives changed as I acquired deeper insight on how people differed from each other. Each of us is born with a basket of unique advantages and limitations. In fact, advantages and limitations are often like the two sides of one coin. Although not always the case, a person who is book-smart tends to be less street-smart, and vice versa.

Every basket has its best place in the world. There is really no better or worse about it, only unique. As I began to see myself holistically, I felt comfortable to accept every-thing about myself. I was in harmony with myself, with all my strengths and weaknesses, and with all my blessings and flaws. I was more excited than ever to discover myself and to become myself.

Drive Self-transformation with Self-honesty

If self-discovery is our starting point, self-transformation is our destination. As much as I was excited to pursue my calling and live a different life, I had many moments of doubts and fears as I explored new things: What if I am not good enough? What if I fail and embarrass myself? What if the change brings risks? During such moments, I would withdraw and find excuses not to move forward. The excuse that I gave most frequently to myself was, "If other people are fine just going through the motions, it's fine for me too."

I was not determined to transform myself until I came across these words of Steve Jobs, which led me to complete self-honesty, "Remembering that I'll be dead soon is the most important tool I've ever encountered to help me make the big choices in life. Almost everything—all external expectations, all pride, all fear of embarrassment or failure—these things just fall away in the face of death, leaving only what is truly important."

It is said that people, in general, can't imagine the moment they will face death. Therefore, "People live as if they are never going to die, and then die having never really lived." After I came across Steve Jobs' words, I meditated on the two questions: How would it feel on the last day and last moment of my life? What would I regret that I had done and I had not done? A little unsettling at first, it was the most profound and mind-altering experience for me.

I suddenly was able to see the big picture. As I vividly sensed the fragility and mortality of life, a life that had always seemed complicated became simple. It was clear that only a few things truly matter when I reach the end of this life, one of which is living up to my full potential. In fact, one of the top regrets people have before they die is not living up to their potential. In order not to have that regret, I must work toward my dreams, regardless of the fears, the embarrassments and the risks.

In an exquisite way, the experience also gave me an opportunity to contemplate the infinity of the soul. I felt peace and freedom to be the person I was designed to be, because I realized that at the end of my life, God is the only one to whom I am ultimately accountable.

Billy Cox, author and speaker, once said, "Self-honesty is the greatest honesty because it leads to all significant change." Many people are stuck in life and unable to transform themselves to the next level, because they are not honest about where they truly are and how they truly feel.

Some hold on to a frustrating career year after year. They tell themselves, "My life is good; I have a decent, stable income." Some tolerate a toxic marriage because they are not willing to become self-sufficient. They tell themselves, "My life is good; I live in a big house, with a huge closet filled with nice clothes." Some face a bleak financial outlook upon retirement. They tell themselves, "My life is good; things will take care of themselves when I retire." Because they are not self-honest, they prefer to make excuses while ignoring or rejecting the opportunities that arise throughout their lives.

Sometimes, one has to be willing to take one step back, in order to get out of a rut and move ten steps forward. To be self-honest, ask yourself these questions: Am I really where I think I am? Am I truly happy with where I am? Can I honestly say that I have lived a wonderful life, with no regrets, at the last day of my life?

It's a lifelong journey to learn about ourselves and to transform ourselves. However, as said by Lao Tzu, the ancient Chinese philosopher, "The journey of a thousand miles begins with one step." The first step I took on the journey was to discover my temperament.

4

Your Temperament is Permanent

Our brain is a sort of computer which has temperament for its hardware and character for its software.
—David Keirsey

Temperament is given to us at conception and involves the aspects of personality—such as introversion vs. extroversion, introspective vs. observant—that are innate rather than learned.

Generally speaking, personality refers to a person's behavioral actions and reactions to daily events in life. When we talk about personality, we may think of any number of descriptions, such as extroverted or introverted, humorous or serious, open or guarded, warm or aloof, quiet or talkative, competitive or collaborative. Our personality is shaped by our inborn temperament and by the environment in which we grow from infancy into adulthood. The inborn temperament, as demonstrated in my stories below, reflects our nature and tends to persist over a lifetime.

After my friend and I watched a movie, she would describe more about the scenes with picture-like details. I would describe more about emotions and thoughts triggered by the scenes. When we walked out of a grocery store, she could easily recall the prices of the asparagus, the steaks and the lobsters. All I could think of was how to enjoy the asparagus, the steaks and the lobsters. It was not because I had money to spare that I didn't pay attention to the prices. It was because I am one of the individuals who are more introspective than observant.

It took me about fifteen minutes to drive between work and home. There was a small cemetery along the way, but it was a little above the ground level and behind the trees. One day, I took a colleague from Asia to lunch. As we passed the cemetery, she pointed at it with surprise, "Wow, they built a cemetery right by the houses?" It caught her attention because in Asian culture, cemeteries are usually located far away from residential areas. I looked at the cemetery in disbelief. I had never noticed it before, and I had driven by it for years!

Discover Your Temperament Type

There are several professional, research based personality/temperament test instruments well established and widely used in the world, such as Myers–Briggs Type Indicator (MBTI), Keirsey Temperament Sorter II (KTS II), and DiSC assessment. Assessing ourselves using one or more of the instruments is a good starting point to understand our personality/temperament. Many of you may have taken some of the assessments through your school or work. I took MBTI and DiSC on several occasions in the past. It was fun and interesting to see the results, but I didn't actually consider their implications in my life.

As I seriously engaged in self-discovery, I revisited my old test results. In addition, I studied the book *Please Understand Me II* by Dr. David Keirsey, the founder of Keirsey Temperament Sorter II. The book includes the temperament sorter which helps identify your temperament type. It also offers comprehensive descriptions of each temperament type as well as the implications of temperament type in various situations in life. In this book, I primarily refer to the results from Keirsey Temperament Sorter II. However, the results from all three test instruments were very insightful. Although there is a high level of consistency, they look at things from somewhat different angles.

Each temperament or personality type has its own unique advantages and challenges. There is really no better or worse about it. Based on Keirsey Temperament Sorter II, I am an "Idealist" in terms of temperament type. Generally speaking, people of this type are more introspective than observant, more friendly than tough-minded, and more people oriented than task oriented.

Furthermore, there are four character types under the temperament type "Idealist." I am at the border line between the character type "Teacher" and "Counselor." "Teacher" type is more of an extrovert and "Counselor" type is more of an introvert. I am more of an ambivert, fairly balanced between introversion and extroversion. Because my goal was to understand myself, instead of fitting into a type, I learned about both types and identified all the characteristics applicable to me.

It gave me goose bumps when I read the first paragraph of the "Idealist" description on the Keirsey website. I couldn't help shouting out, "Wow, this is me!" It felt like there was a virtual friend. The friend saw a theme in my life through what I experienced as fragmented and random events. The friend articulated what I felt inside—but couldn't express—with unparalleled clarity and comprehensiveness. The paragraph went like this:

> "Idealists are passionately concerned with personal growth and development. Idealists strive to discover who they are and how they can become their best possible self—always this quest for self-knowledge and

self-improvement drives their imagination. And they want to help others make the journey. Idealists are naturally drawn to working with people, and whether in education or counseling, in social services or personnel work, in journalism or the ministry, they are gifted at helping others find their way in life, often inspiring them to grow as individuals and to fulfill their potentials."

Although the paragraph describes me fairly well, it should be recognized that no test or theory can ever perfectly depict the temperament or personality at an individual level. Everyone is unique even under the same type. "Guardian," the most common type out of the four temperament types, accounts for about 40-45% of the population. In spite of their commonalities, every Guardian is different in their own ways.

That's why self-reflection is important as we interpret the test results. Personally, when I answered the temperament sorter questionnaire, I reflected on the specific stories, events, and patterns in my life as related to each question. As I studied the descriptions of my own types as well as other types, I also asked myself, "How do I see myself similar to or different from these descriptions?"

Connect the Dots into Patterns

As I went through this process, a lot of the things in my life that seemed random in the past started to make sense and show a pattern. I used to live through them but not think about them. As I became aware, I was able to harness the power of the awareness and make my life more enjoyable and more fulfilling.

I enjoy interesting, inspiring, meaningful conversations, whether with friends or with new people that I meet in different settings. These conversations invigorate me and replenish me with fresh perspectives which can be easily eroded by the routines in life. One of my favorite ways to pass time is to enjoy a nice conversation, accompanied by a cup of tea or coffee. However, I never gave much thought to the interest until I learned that this specific interest was characteristic of my "Idealist" temperament.

As I became aware of it, I made several refinements in my life. I am not a party person but I host parties occasionally. I either do small parties with one or two families, or do large parties when there is a topic or purpose. This enables me to connect with everyone in a deeper and more meaningful way.

As I continue to explore and pursue my calling, I have had many opportunities to engage in-depth and meaningful conversations with others. It truly makes my work feel as play.

Meanwhile, I learned that my preference for non-fiction books was also typical of my temperament, as "Idealists" were driven to learn and to improve. Being an avid reader, I make an effort to read books of various genres. However, whenever I am in a library or in a bookstore, the section I am naturally drawn to is always non-fiction. When I had just completed college, I worked briefly as a magazine editor. I had a large office with rows of bookshelves, filled with classic non-fiction literature. It was the best part of the job that I still miss.

Some nonfiction books are always fun to read and easy to apply, such as the books related to lifestyle, personal style and parenting. The other nonfiction books are more intellectually engaging, such as the books related to business, psychology and behavioral science. These books often inspired interesting thoughts and ideas in my mind, but even as I read and learned, I had a nagging feeling that these thoughts and ideas were locked inside of me, like a pond of water that didn't flow anywhere. Sometimes I wondered why I couldn't relax and entertain myself with more light-hearted fiction books.

I was able to look at my preference from a new perspective after I learned that it was a natural reflection of my drive to help myself and others grow, as embedded in my "Idealist" temperament. I realized that I should proactively seek opportunities to express this side of me, instead of doubting the value of my interest and passively accepting the limitations imposed by my situations. I was once again reminded of the sparkles that had flashed in my heart from time to time—the desire to help others achieve their potential.

Reignite the Sparkles in Your Dreams

I had been interested in coaching and development for many years. Long before I started my MBA program, I researched the profession extensively, prompted by the tiny sparkles flashing in my heart. However, the research didn't lead to any actions because it seemed to be too big of a leap to change from finance to a coaching and development profession. The gap was so intimidating that I backed out without even trying.

I knew my reluctance to try was caused by my lack of confidence more than lack of means. At the time, without clear self-knowledge, I didn't have the conviction that it would be the right path for me although it seemed to be my dream and passion. Therefore, I chose to stay in my comfort zone and on the path of least resistance.

As I learned about my temperament, I saw the connections between my temperament, my love for meaningful conversations, my love for nonfiction books and my passion for self-development and the development of others. The sparkles were rekindled in my heart. I felt a fresh sense of confidence, which was further solidified as I discovered my natural talents, passions and aligned these with my core values. The confidence propelled me to take actions and ultimately made my dream come true.

Today you may be putting your dreams on hold just as I did many years ago. You have felt the sparkle in your heart but never managed to turn that sparkle into flame, because you are unsure. If you are in this situation, you may greatly benefit from discovering your temperament as well as the other traits being mentioned in this book.

As I discovered my own temperament, I also learned more about the other types of temperament, which offered valuable insight into why other people behaved differently from myself, and how we could leverage each other's strength to achieve common goals. I began to appreciate and embrace diversity at a much deeper level.

Temperament in Organizations

In addition to its implications in an individual's life, temperament also has important implications in organizational development. I am a feeling-oriented person, often described by my friends and coworkers as pleasant, friendly and easy going. At one time, I was asked to take on a project manager role in a large, complex project at work. In this role, I needed to develop a proposal based on the input of people from different functions and regions. I then needed to drive buy-in on the proposal from the same group of people.

Unfortunately, our meetings were filled with conflicts and heated arguments. Everyone had different opinions and passionately defended their own positions. I understood that we had to move forward, but I was uncomfortable with the thought of hurting someone's feelings. I painstakingly came up with many versions of proposals, trying to reflect everyone's input as much as I could. It turned out to be a futile exercise because it was impossible to accommodate the many conflicting opinions in any one proposal.

To make a long story short, we were not able to meet the project deadline. I was frustrated as I had never missed deadlines or goals in the past. The frustration was accompanied by stress and embarrassment. We decided to bring in an experienced project manager at that point. With a personality opposite to mine, she was distinctly task oriented. She decisively subdued the noises that weren't leading the project anywhere and quickly moved the project forward. As I humbly watched her in action, I realized how much time and energy I had spent to accommodate everyone's feelings!

Personally, I learned a lot from this experience, and have since learned the skills of handling conflicts. The experience also taught me the importance of matching the person and the task in organizations. When a feeling-oriented person is placed in a situation that demands a task-oriented personality, or vice versa, it usually leads to less effective business results.

If an organization understands its members' temperaments and talents, strengths and limitations, and places people in the most suitable roles, both the organization and its members can greatly benefit from it. Many organizations have introduced temperament testing as part of their talent management process and as a way to improve productivity.

As a team member, you can add value to your organization by proactively understanding your own temperament, talents and passions, and then seeking opportunities where your natural gifts can best serve you and your organization.

Overcome Cultural Bias

I am an ambivert who demonstrates introvert and extrovert tendencies fairly evenly. My extrovert tendency has been primarily demonstrated in my childhood and in situations out of classroom and office; while my introvert tendency has been primarily demonstrated in classroom and in office, probably because the environment is more structured.

My introvert side emerged as a teenager. I enjoyed interacting with my friends. I could present myself comfortably when I needed to or when I liked to. But I preferred to be quiet and reserved otherwise. Because I acted as a practical introvert in many situations, I was aware of the biases and disadvantages that introverts often experienced.

Compared to social butterflies, wall flowers have more challenges moving upward in traditional organizations. Psychologically, there is a "mere exposure effect"—the tendency to develop a preference for people or things merely because of familiarity. If you rarely "fly" before the people higher above, you tend to be less recognized and have less opportunities.

Culturally, we live in a society that favors extrovert qualities, with a particular obsession with leadership. Although leadership can be interpreted and demonstrated in many different ways, the leadership qualities that the society typically defines are demonstrated more often in extroverts than in introverts.

In organizations, group work is exalted and often mistaken as teamwork. In the dictionary, teamwork is defined as "the combined action of a group of people, especially when *effective and efficient*." It's not any kind of group work. Many studies have shown that higher quality ideas are generated when people work alone instead of in a group, such as the Diehl & Stroebe study, conducted by German psychologist Michael Diehl and Wolfgang Stroebe.

Naturally, extroverts prefer to work in a group; while introverts prefer to work alone. Introverts can be great team players when it's meaningful to work as a team. In fact, introverts often foster teamwork more effectively because of their listening skills. However, they can feel burdened if they have to work in a group just for the sake of it. Sometimes it's hard for introverts to admit this as they may be labeled as poor team players.

The great qualities of introverts, such as focused, independent, good listener, are often undervalued compared to the extrovert qualities. However, introverts can become highly successful individuals and leaders in life. Warren Buffet, Bill Gates, and author J.K. Rowling are a few examples among the many successful introverts. If you are an introvert or a worried parent of an introvert child, I would recommend you read the book, *Quiet: The Power of Introverts in a World That Can't Stop Talking,* authored by Susan Cain. You may gain a fresh perspective.

As a personal philosophy, I try to focus on what I can control or change in life, instead of complaining about what I can't control or change, such as culture or society. Everyone has an ideal place in the world where their personalities can be advantageous. Our mission is to discover that ideal place. Although my introvert tendency limits my development in some areas, my ambivert nature gives me an edge in fostering deeper understanding of and connections with others. It has been a key success factor in pursuing my calling of helping others.

Introversion or extroversion is a matter of natural preferences in the way we interact with the environment. Neither of the tendencies is responsible for non-productive mindset or behaviors. I used to consider my shyness as an expression of my introvert side, but later I realized that for me and for many others, shyness was actually rooted in the fear of rejections and the fear of judgment.

These fears occur in both introverts and extroverts. They are only expressed differently. In fact, a lot of introverts are not shy at all and are fully capable of dealing effectively with others' opinions. Abraham Lincoln and Mahatma Gandhi are examples that come to mind. You may want to examine if you are associating negative, non-productive behaviors or mindset with your own temperament. Most likely they are not part of your nature, but more based on your past experiences.

Caveats to Watch For

As we discover our temperament, as well as other inborn traits, we want to avoid the trap of labeling ourselves, especially labeling us as incompetent in the areas that don't come frequently and naturally to us. Although we demonstrate some tendencies more frequently and naturally, we are multifaceted as human beings. Some of the most lively and entertaining people on stage or on screen are very quiet and private in their personal lives.

Although I am generally more introspective than observant, I am very observant when I choose to pay attention. I clearly remember the many public posters I saw in the Hong Kong MTR subways. The posters were simple, warm and charming, reflecting the perfect harmony between the vintage and the modern side of Hong Kong.

I remember a poster with a little vintage style Chinese poem praising passengers with good manners. Two cute cartoon children were drawn besides the poem. They both had round, apple-like faces, bending forward with their thumbs up, with a lovely, humble smile on their faces. I remember the words and drawings in the poster even today.

Another trap to avoid is to expect a world tailored perfectly for who we are. As we plan our work and life, we want to make them aligned with our natural temperament as much as possible. It makes life more enjoyable and more productive. People of "Idealist" temperament type thrive in a harmonious environment rather than a highly-charged environment filled with conflicts and politics. Naturally, I would choose a harmonious environment for myself as much as I can.

However, conflicts are natural occurrences in life. They can't be eliminated even in the most harmonious environment. Conflict management is a skill that we all can acquire through learning and practice. Although it's not in my nature, I learned to be steadfast when I chose to deal with a conflict. I was able to focus on overarching goals and solutions, being assertive in expressing my own views while respecting others' views.

Although temperament is permanent, it can be a positive force for each of us. Once we understand it, we can make choices based on it, focus on our strengths and respond effectively to challenges. Throughout the self-discovery journey, we want to always keep in mind that the purpose of self-discovery is not to label or restrict ourselves, but to develop and empower ourselves.

5

Your Priceless Natural Talents

When I stand before God, at the end of my life, I would
hope that I would not have a single bit of talent left—and
could say—I used everything you gave me.
—*Erma Bombeck*

Natural talents are the talents we received in our DNA, such
as musical affinity, color perception, finger dexterity. They
offer us advantages in life by helping us learn and do certain
things more easily and quickly, Natural talents have little to
do with the training and education we are exposed to
throughout our lives. They are part of our genetic
inheritance, similar to our inborn physical characteristics
and temperament.

Some people are naturally better at performing certain
activities than others. My friend Linda has always
demonstrated a great sense of space. She is able to visualize
vividly in three dimensions. She also has an eye for seeing
things in perspective and balance. When she walks into a
room, she can immediately see even if a painting is just a
hair away from being perfectly leveled.

She has lived in a few new homes since I met her. Without any formal architectural training, she custom designed and built each home from scratch. First, she would make sketches of the entire home, room by room, based on the three-dimensional picture she already saw in her mind. Her husband Harold, an engineer by training, would then scale up her sketches into a formal drawing.

I visited her home frequently when we lived in Houston. Her home was beautiful and highly functional, with meticulous details and design elements working precisely for her and Harold's needs. Even their light switches were positioned according to her and Harold's height!

She enjoys decorating a home too. When she looks at a piece of furniture or artifact, she sees exactly how it would fit in the room, instantly and accurately. She once helped me select a couch and a picture frame. I was so nervous as they looked huge. As it turned out, they fit just right in my living room. When she recently moved into a new home, she picked a spot for the piano. Harold thought there was no way to fit the piano there. Again, you can imagine who was right. Linda didn't acquire her spatial aptitude through learning. It was just inherent in her, naturally.

Being opposite to Linda, I have a poor sense of space. We moved many times before settling down in our present home. Every time when we looked for a new place, I had to diligently measure everything and lay out the measurements on the floor to physically see how our furniture would fit, because I was unable to visualize how things fit in my mind.

If I skipped this step, surprises always arose. I remember my anxieties when the furniture arrived: Why did the sofa look so awkward there? Why did that chandelier appear so big in the room? Why was there no room to fit in the other side table?... I, of course, wouldn't dream of building a new home in the way Linda did. With my level of spatial aptitude, it would cause me too much anxiety.

Your Talents May Not Appear Spectacular

Somehow it seemed much easier for me to recognize my natural ineptitudes than natural aptitudes. I could easily identify what I was not good at, such as the sense of space and athletics. However, I had a hard time identifying what I was naturally good at.

In my humble view, it would be self-glorifying and boastful to claim a talent if I didn't demonstrate any extraordinary abilities or achievements. We all would agree that Mozart had musical talent and Shakespeare had writing talent. But what could I say about me, someone who had hardly won any trophies growing up?

The truth is, natural talent doesn't always demonstrate itself in a spectacular way. The level of a natural talent differs among virtually all people. It may fall anywhere on the scale from slightly above average to far beyond average, as with a prodigy. Professional assessment may give us an idea about where some of our natural talents are on the scale.

Talents may or may not lead to great accomplishments. Some people may be committed to develop their talents to the highest possible level; some people may only polish their talents to some extent; some people may never even be aware of their talents.

Our natural talents enable us to acquire certain skills more rapidly, and with less practice or hard work, compared to average people. No matter where they are on the scale and to which extent we develop them, our talents are always there.

How Natural Talents Impact Performance

Natural talents have significant impact on our enjoyment, fulfillment, and success in life. When we use our natural talents, in a hobby or in a career, we learn faster and progress faster. When our natural talent is expressed as an interest or passion, we are more likely to experience the wonderful feeling of "flow" or "zone," the mental state of being fully immersed in energized focus, intense involvement and deep enjoyment.

Natural talents alone don't lead to high performance unless we develop them into abilities. Our abilities depend on natural talents and many other factors, such as the level of interest, the time and effort invested, the quality of training and education, the role models or mentors we have in life.

Certain abilities depend more on natural talents, such as athletic abilities, music abilities, structural visualization abilities and analytical abilities. Even with a lot of knowledge and skill practices, these abilities are more difficult to cultivate without natural talents in our genetic makeup.

In professional careers that heavily rely on these abilities, especially highly competitive and high-performance driven careers, natural talent is a key determinant for success as the level of natural talent implies a ceiling, the maximum potential or highest possible level of performance that an individual can attain.

Natural talents, as well as body structure, are essential to high performance in most Olympic sports. It's not unusual for top coaches in these fields to only look for candidates with highly promising raw talents to work with. For a young boy or girl who dreams of being an Olympic athlete, the fulfillment of the dream will have to depend on natural talents as well as body's biomechanical structure, not only desire and dedication.

In the recruiting process, most organizations rely on education and years of experience to determine a candidate's professional qualification, with little consideration of natural talent or potential. However, absent of a highly relevant natural talent, a person with the required education and experiences could still end up not performing.

During my finance career, I have seen financial analysts who were "well qualified" otherwise, but unfortunately lacked analytical aptitude. They struggled to deliver the expected performance, especially having a hard time analyzing complex business problems. In spite of my degree in Information Systems, I lack the aptitude essential for a good programmer. If I were to hire a programmer, I would rather not hire myself, but hire a high potential individual talented at and passionate about programming, even without an advanced degree.

Other abilities depend on natural talents but to a lesser extent, especially the soft skills such as emotional intelligence, communication and leadership. Soft skills are crucial to success across different professions and trades. Given positive role models, mentors and coaches, there is much more room to cultivate these skills if one is willing to improve.

I have a high school classmate who was quiet and shy at school. I could never have imagined that one day she would become the mayor of our prospering town. When I visited China last year, I met her at a high school classmates' reunion. At our dinner table, it was evident that over the years, she had totally transformed herself in terms of her communication, leadership and maturity level. I was more than impressed. If she could transform like that, so could you and I.

Knowing our natural talents and their implications enhances our ability to live a more enjoyable and fulfilling life. From a career perspective, it enables us to make more educated career decisions, and potentially achieve greater success in life.

Discover Your Natural Talents

To discover my natural talents, I first reflected on a series of self-discovery questions.

Some of the most helpful questions to me were:

- 🦋 What do I see myself doing better or worse compared to the others?
- 🦋 What was I recognized for as a child and as an adult?
- 🦋 What did people tell me that I was gifted in as a child and as an adult?
- 🦋 What kind of activities do I enjoy, to a point where I lose track of time?
- 🦋 What can I do well naturally without much training?

A few things came to my mind as I reflected on these questions. I did well academically, and I was good at the analytical work at my jobs. When I was a child, I enjoyed debating activities. People commented that I should become a lawyer or a journalist when I grew up. Therefore, I may have some level of natural talents in reasoning, analytical, information processing and language ability.

To further discover my talents. I turned to several professional resources. The Johnson O'Connor Research Foundation and The Ball Foundation are two of the leading aptitude research and assessment organizations in the United States. The Johnson O'Connor Research Foundation defines aptitudes as "... natural talents, special abilities for doing, or learning to do, certain kinds of things easily and quickly. They have little to do with knowledge or culture, or education, or even interests. They have to do with heredity."

Following the definition, the organization offers aptitude assessment that covers a comprehensive list of aptitudes, including Structural Visualization, Inductive Reasoning, Ideaphoria, Graphoria, Analytical Reasoning, Numerical Aptitudes, Auditory Aptitudes, Silograms, Memory for Design & Observation, Color Discrimination, Visual Designs, Dexterities, Foresight, Word Association and English Vocabulary.

The Johnson O'Connor Research Foundation published an electronic book *Understanding Your Aptitudes*, available on its website. It is well written and includes comprehensive descriptions, stories, and application guides about each of the aptitudes. You can gain a lot of valuable insight from the book. If you don't take the aptitude assessment, however, it is unlikely to accurately assess where you are on the scale in terms of each talent.

I then looked into Clifton StrengthsFinder, developed by Dr. Donald O. Clifton, the former Gallup chairman and the "Father of Strengths-Based Psychology" as named by the American Psychological Association. The strength is defined slightly different from natural talent in that the strength emphasizes the ability to consistently perform at a top level. However, as recognized by the Gallup research, although talents, skills, knowledge are each important for building a strength, natural talent is always the most important of all.

According to the Gallup research, people who use their strengths every day, are six times more likely to be fully engaged in their work. The Clifton StrengthsFinder measures and ranks the presence of 34 talent themes or strengths. The more dominant a talent theme is in a person, the more the theme impacts the person's performance.

Another good read is the book *Frames of Mind: The Theory of Multiple Intelligences*, authored by psychologist Dr. Howard Gardner. In his book, Dr. Howard Gardner identified multiple types of intelligences, such as logical-mathematical, verbal-linguistic, musical-rhythmic, visual-spatial, bodily-kinesthetic, interpersonal, intrapersonal, naturalistic etc.

Although our education system still predominantly judges a child's smartness by the Intelligence Quotient (IQ), it is now widely recognized that the traditional view of IQ based intelligence has been too narrow and that there are many types of intelligences beyond IQ.

The aptitudes research, the strengths research, and the multiple intelligence theory, although from different viewpoints, all converge to one point: there are many different kinds of talents or intelligences and none of them is inherently superior to the others. Although the research mentioned above has identified an extensive list of common strengths or natural talents, there are many other natural talents that people may possibly possess.

As you think of your natural talents, be open-minded and carefully observe all the possible gifts you have been given. Some people are very sensitive to smells or tastes. Although these aptitudes are not covered by the typical aptitude assessment, the special ability of smell or taste discrimination can make successful careers as perfumers or wine tasters. The self-reflection questions mentioned earlier may help you discover these unusual talents.

Choose Professional Testing for Your Purpose

As you face different aptitude test options, you may want to choose based on your specific goals and the specific aptitudes you are interested in measuring. Because I already had a specific career aspiration in helping others develop and grow, I was mainly looking for a test to confirm the aspiration. I decided to take the Clifton StrengthsFinder because the talent themes it measures were more relevant to my career aspiration.

Based on the Clifton StrengthsFinder, out of the 34 themes being measured, my top five talent themes are: connectedness—"faith, benevolence and acceptance rooted in the sense of connection among all mankind and all things;" maximizer—"the ability to focus on and capitalize the strengths of self and others to reach excellence;" empathy—"the ability to understand others' feeling and to help others express the feelings;" intellection— "introspective and appreciate thinking and intellectual discussions;" futuristic—"focus on what could be in the future, and inspire self and others with the vision of the future."

The result was eye opening to me. Although I did experience these talent themes in my life, I never recognized them as my talents or strengths, because they were not as obvious as some "demonstrative talents." Running is an example of "demonstrative talent." You can easily recognize a running talent based on your results in a track meet. But you can't recognize some other talents as easily. This is one of reasons why it's difficult to discover natural talents by self-reflection alone.

The five talent themes were relevant and supportive to my career aspiration. Discovering my natural talents gave me a brand-new way of looking at myself. I saw much potential in myself which I had never seen before. I no longer felt regret for the talents that I didn't have, such as athletic talent, as I realized what a wonderful basket of gifts I had been given.

Although I didn't take an aptitude test offered by Johnson O'Connor Research Foundation or The Ball Foundation, high school students considering college majors and college students preparing to enter the work force may be ideal candidates for the test. Many adults also choose to test themselves when they are considering a job or career change or when they are facing the possibility of downsizing or early retirement.

An advantage of the aptitude test is that it is not based on answers to questionnaires and reports of self-perceptions, but based on how well one actually can perform a particular task. The results you receive are more objective. Of course, the cost is also higher. A comprehensive aptitude test can cost a few hundred dollars as it involves several hours of hands-on activities and professional reviews; however, the benefit could last a lifetime.

Live Like a Bird Flying with the Wind

If we choose a professional career which demands a highly relevant natural talent, it's better to make sure we have the natural talents, so that we can live like a bird flying with the wind, not against the wind.

There is no doubt that persistence and hard work can accomplish a great deal even in the absence of an essential natural talent. However, sometimes we may want to take a step back and ask: Is the result achieved under the condition sustainable and scalable in the long run? More importantly, is it worth the pains and sufferings to accomplish something that we are neither good at nor passionate about, when we could have pursued something that we are much better at and genuinely passionate about?

Some parents, eager for their children to become high achievers, push and pressure their children to achieve impressive performance, even in activities where the children apparently lack natural talent. This higher performance may last until their early adulthood. However, it is often not sustainable without the underlying natural talent. As mentioned earlier, many people, in spite of their advanced education and years of experiences, do not succeed in their field due to lack of an intrinsic talent.

I read a poignant story about a family, where the parents were highly accomplished attorneys, but the daughter, unfortunately, was not blessed with her parents' particular intelligence. However, the mother was determined to make her daughter successful in the same profession. With the mother's insistence, her daughter made it into law school. But her performance slipped quickly in college because her mom couldn't be there to push her and help her. Nonetheless, after graduation, she entered a top law firm because of her mother's personal influence.

To everyone's shock, she committed suicide soon after she started her career. In the letter she left to her mom, she said, "Mom, I am so tired, for all these years... as much as I try, I can't do my job. I don't want to disappoint you, but I don't want to live like this anymore..." I was so sad as I read the story. I couldn't help wondering how differently things could've turned out if the mom could have helped her daughter discover a path aligned with her natural talents. I am sure she had her unique talents as everyone did, but she never had the opportunity to sing her own song.

The other story that I deeply identified with was about a lady named Sonya, as appeared in the electronic book *Understanding Your Aptitudes* published by the Johnson O'Connor Research Foundation. Sonya was high on the aptitude Foresight, and low on the aptitude Structural Visualization.

Briefly, Structural Visualization is the ability to visualize in three dimensions. It aids occupations such as Engineering, Architecture and Computer Programming. Foresight is the ability to see possibilities, which often lead people to be persistent in their pursuits. Persistence is a highly valuable quality essential to any success. However, persistence may lead to disappointments if it is applied in the wrong direction as in Sonya's case.

Sonya was persistent in pursuing an education and then a career in Structural Engineering, in which unfortunately, she did not display natural talent. Although the path was very difficult and unnatural for her, she persisted to prove her own intellectual capacity. After ten years of frustrations, she took an aptitude test and finally recognized, "Though seeing possibilities is a gift, persistence only works if it takes you to a place that is natural."

Like Sonya, I am also lower in Structural Visualization and higher on Foresight. I enrolled in a Master's Program in Information Systems and jumped on the information technology bandwagon in 1999, because it was hot and popular and most of my friends were on the bandwagon. Both the university and the program I attended had excellent reputations. My professors and classmates were wonderful to work with. However, I quickly realized that I was neither talented at nor interested in programming.

Still, I persisted in getting my master's degree. I was only luckier than Sonya in that I didn't enter the information technology profession, and instead, stayed with my finance career in which I was relatively talented.

Many people live in a mode of high resistance at work, like a bird flying against the wind, struggling to make up for the absence of an essential natural talent. Sometimes they impulsively select college majors for which they are not suited, because some family members or friends recommended these majors. Sometimes they select their professions based upon money and status, rather than long term opportunities and genuine fulfillment. Sometimes they are trapped by the unrealistic expectations of others, like the daughter who was caught in the unrealistic expectations of her successful attorney mom.

Life is short. There has to be a better way to live. If you choose a professional career, and it requires the kind of abilities difficult to cultivate without an underlying natural talent, it's better to make sure you have the natural talent. Fly with the wind; do not fly against the wind.

What If "I Don't Have Much Talent?"

In a profession where a natural talent is a key success factor, it's preferred that we have that natural talent. Lack of a particular talent can be a reason to fail in a particular profession, however, it is never an excuse to fail in life.

In-depth testing demonstrates again and again that we all have natural talents. There are more than enough career options for every type of natural talents. I may not succeed as an athlete, a computer programmer, or an architect, but with the talents I have, I can succeed in a financial analysis career or a career that helps people develop and grow.

There are also sufficient career options for every level of natural talents. Not everyone is destined to be an Olympic champion. People with moderate athletic talents can enjoy successful careers in coaching, teaching or sports management. I read about a man who was absolutely passionate about golf. He competed in his younger years but didn't go far due to lack of talent. He changed direction and built a successful consulting business serving professional golf players. He was happy and fulfilled, without being confined by his lack of golfing talent.

None of my own natural talents is at a prodigy level. Although I don't have ribbons or medals collected in a box to impress my children, what matters to me is whether I express and enjoy my moderate talents to their fullest. As beautifully said by Leo Buscaglia, "Our talent is God's gift to us. What we do with it is our gift back to God." Each of us is a champion as long as we give our best to express and enjoy the gifts given to us.

We want to be open-minded and keep a growth mindset in every area of our life. Even with a lack of natural talent, we can still get better at something if we have strong, intrinsic desire to improve and we are willing to invest time and effort in it. Although I was not born with a good sense of style, I was determined to improve because it was an essential life skill I must live with and deal with every day.

Of course, even with my enthusiasm and dedication, I would not expect myself to become a professional stylist. Without the intuitive sense of style, it would be difficult for me to create and improvise impressive looks. However, I could manage to style myself securely and confidently by following a set of proven principles. I figured that, on a scale of 1 to 10, there was at least potential to raise my style to a 5 with learning and practice, even if I could not raise it to a 10.

Sometimes we use "I don't have much talent" as an excuse for avoiding chores and responsibilities. I used to consider cooking as boring and burdensome. I used this line as an excuse for doing little cooking. The truth is, most of the mandatory chores and responsibilities in life are not high performance driven. They don't need so much natural talent. Yes, a top chef needs a special gift in cooking, but everyone can learn how to cook basic, healthy food with basic training.

I became interested in cooking later in my life. After I had children, I realized that cooking and housework in general, like personal style, were important life management skills to master for boys and girls alike. These skills directly impact our quality of life. Some families are well-to-do, but they live a messy, and unhealthy life. Some families, even with modest means, live a neat, cozy and healthy life. Admittedly not best at these skills, I am committed to keep getting better at them.

Sometimes we use "I don't have much talent" as an excuse for accepting the status quo and refusing to change. Although certain professional success requires specific natural talent, many highly successful individuals don't have extraordinary natural talents or advanced education. What sets them apart are other success factors such as their vision, passion, attitude, and mindset, which can all be cultivated with commitment. More often than not, they also know how to collaborate and leverage others' talents to collectively reach success.

Mega Talent: Talent of Leveraging Talents

One of the classic stories about the talent of leveraging talents involves the "smartest ignorant man" Henry Ford, the founder of the Ford Motor Company. During World War I, a newspaper publicly attacked Ford's intelligence as he had little formal education. The case was brought to court. At the court proceedings, the newspaper's lawyers tried to prove Ford's ignorance by asking him a series of questions on history and philosophy.

"They basically asked him, you might say, high school questions," historian John Stadenmaier said in the PBS documentary *Henry Ford*. "And he was revealed to be pathetically inarticulate and ill-informed. The stuff he didn't know was amazing to people." As the questions became too much, Ford finally attacked back,

"If I should really want to answer the foolish questions you have just asked, or any of the other questions you have been asking me, let me remind you that I have a row of electric push-buttons on my desk, and by pushing the right button, I can summon to my aid men who can answer any question I desire concerning the business to which I am devoting most of my efforts. Now, will you kindly tell me, why I should clutter up my mind with general knowledge, for the purpose of being able to answer questions, when I have men around me who can supply any knowledge I require?"

The lawyers were speechless at the statement. Henry Ford won the lawsuit with a 6-cent verdict.

In today's world, collaboration and leveraging extend far beyond the vertical situations between boss and subordinates, as it was in Ford's case. They often happen horizontally in a mutually beneficial partnership or network, where people can add value to each other with their unique talents.

We can rarely accomplish a great mission singlehandedly, because one person's talent is limited, no matter how great it is. Imagine you are a scientist. You are passionate about commercializing your invention, so that it can truly benefit the world. But your talent is in research, and you have little talent in marketing and sales. Should you stop pursuing your passion? Of course not, because you can engage people with talents in marketing and sales to collectively accomplish this mission.

I have been fortunate to collaborate with teams of diverse talents in several areas of my life. A great team not only shares the common visions and goals, but also recognizes, respects and strategically leverages each team member's talents and strengths. When everyone's talents are properly utilized, together the team can generate powerful compound effects and accomplish far more than the sum of what each individual can accomplish alone.

Many smart people are not able to accomplish much in life because they are not able to collaborate. They lose sight of their goals and allow their personalities to become roadblocks to success. As a result, they become talent repellent rather than talent attractor, and collaboration killer rather than collaboration facilitator.

It's especially challenging for a few types of people to collaborate with others. Some habitually focus on their strengths and others' weaknesses. Some are close-minded and assume they are always right. Some are over controlling and must monitor others' every step. Some are egotistical and can't tolerate others to shine. Some are insecure, suspicious and generally have issues in trusting others.

To develop a collaborative mindset is beyond a skill development. It involves self-development to cultivate the positive qualities that foster collaboration, such as open-mindedness, respect, gratitude, generosity, trust.

It would be wonderful if each of us could live like a bird flying with the wind, doing the things in which we are naturally talented, and using both our wings and the currents to take us higher than we ever thought possible. It would be even more wonderful, if we could collaborate with a team and build the powerful "mega talent."

Enjoy the Best of Your Times

The future has arrived ahead of schedule, at a speed we never could have anticipated. A new technological invention or innovation is announced every five minutes. New developments in automation, communication and artificial intelligence are obsoleting the old ways of doing things.

Knowledge is becoming obsolete at a speed faster than at any time in history. Most of us have experienced firsthand how fast the computer and internet technology have changed. However, the trend is permeating more fields than we may imagine. A Harvard Business Review article, "Be Forewarned: Your Knowledge is Decaying," noted that in the fields of liver disease, such as hepatitis and cirrhosis, half of the knowledge had become obsolete in about 45 years.

Rapid knowledge obsolescence is also accompanied by the explosive speed of knowledge growth. According to the "Knowledge Doubling Curve" created by Buckminster Fuller, human knowledge doubled approximately every century until 1900. By the end of World War II knowledge was doubling every 25 years. Today, on average, knowledge is doubling every 13 months. According to IBM, new internet technology will lead to the doubling of knowledge every 12 hours.

As intimidating as the trend appears to be, history always seems to reflect Charles Dickens' famous opening lines in his classic novel, *A Tale of Two Cities*, "It was the best of times; it was the worst of times." For each individual, whether it is the best or the worst of times depends on how we respond to the essential questions of the current age. Today, the essential question has changed from "What do you know?" to "How fast can you learn?" and furthermore, "How creative can you become?"

This is the best of times for people who clearly understand their unique natural gifts, as they are best equipped to respond to the essential questions of this age. The more aligned your natural talents, as well as your temperament, passions, and values, are with your work, the faster you will learn, the more creative you will be, and the more likely you will succeed in the future. For people gifted and interested in new technologies, the technology changes excite them instead of overwhelming them. They would be the earliest adopters of new technologies, or even better, the group of people creating the new technologies.

In the past, the need for a formal education was a barrier for many people to develop and apply their natural talents. However, technologies today have offered unprecedented education opportunities that are accessible, convenient, and inexpensive. Much knowledge can be obtained through the internet and other platforms. Virtually all the libraries in existence can be downloaded in the palms of our hands. It has never been easier to develop your natural talents and pursue your passion through self-education.

When he was a teenager, Jack Andraka invented a pancreatic cancer detection method. Besides his amazing talent, an incredible part of his story was that most of his learning and research were self-motivated and achieved through internet resources, such as Google, Wikipedia, and free online scientific journals.

His story exemplifies the true meaning of the word "education," rooted from the Latin word "educere" and meant to "draw out what lies within." For centuries, education has primarily followed a rigid form of pushing knowledge from outside in. The trend of the future could nudge education to revert to its authentic roots and to achieve its highest purpose, which is to draw out everyone's natural gifts.

Regardless of your natural talents, I would strongly encourage you to invest some education in liberal arts and humanities subjects, such as literature, art, history, behavioral science and psychology. According to a report released by the Association of American Colleges and Universities, 74% of business and non-profit leaders recommend liberal education in order for one to succeed in today's global economy.

I don't mention this because these subjects are my favorites, but because these subjects nurture qualities that are applicable across all ages, all professions and all aspects of life, such as character, perspective, creativity, imagination, leadership, communication, emotional intelligence, and spiritual intelligence. These qualities are timeless and fundamentally distinguish human beings from computers and robots. Together with our unique natural gifts, they are essential to maintain our competitive advantage as machines take over more and more job functions in the global workforce.

Each of us is endowed with more natural talents than we could fully develop in several lifetimes. Your talents may or may not make you rich in a material sense. However, by discovering and mining your talents, some of which you probably are not even aware that you possess, you will break through to experience unexpected, new levels of enjoyment and fulfillment, which are the most valuable riches of all.

Explore your priceless natural talents with eager anticipation. You owe it to yourself.

6

Finding Passion in Your Purpose

One person with passion is better than
forty people merely interested.
—*E.M. Forster*

Before we explore our passions, we want to have a better understanding of interests as many of us are advised to follow our interests as we make choices in life. The advice has a lot of wisdom. Interests make our life fun and enjoyable. Interests also trigger curiosity and the inner motivation that fuel us to learn, to work, and to succeed. However, there are some caveats about interests.

Interests Can Be Capricious

Interests can be fickle, capricious and unpredictable. Unlike natural talents that are inborn and stay with us all our life, interests can be inspired and influenced by many environmental factors, such as family, friends, and exposure through reading and media. They may or may not be aligned with our natural talents. They may remain strong for a long time or may be fleeting. They may be triggered intrinsically or extrinsically.

Many of us naturally associate interests with natural talents. While they are closely associated, natural talents and interests do not always overlap. A natural talent doesn't necessarily lead to an interest. One may be interested in developing some talents more than the others. A boy born with both an artistic talent and an engineering mind may be interested in engineering, and not interested in art. An interest is not always based on a natural talent either. In spite of my lack of bodily/kinesthetic aptitude, I became interested in dancing from time to time because of its health benefits.

Interests can come easily and flee easily. Although not always the case, people tend to continue their interests in the things they are naturally good at, because their innate talent makes the activity more fun and interesting. If you have bodily/kinesthetic aptitude, you're likely to be interested in sports as you would do much better and have more fun in sports than someone without the aptitude. Unless there is a strong motivation behind it, an interest not based on aptitude is likely to be a fleeting interest.

I don't even remember how many fleeting interests I have ever had. I became interested in sewing many years ago. Just before I was going to part with a pile of ill-fitting pants, I thought it would be cool if I could alter the pants to a perfect fit. I bought a sewing machine and a few books on sewing pants. I successfully altered a pair of pants to a perfect shape. Unfortunately, I couldn't sew in smooth lines, which caused tiny puckers here and there.

I eventually abandoned the project. I knew I wouldn't be able to do a perfect alteration without a great deal of practice. I was better off to buy perfectly fitting pants in the first place. The only useful thing I sewed was a simple toy for my daughters—a three-inch square cloth pack filled with dried corn kernels. They loved to play with it in the backyard, throwing it at each other and counting who got hit the most. Although I gave up the interest, sewing was nevertheless a fun experience, and I definitely learned a few more things about pants!

The few interests that have stayed with me include reading, music, art and theater. When I lived in Philadelphia, I liked to go to New York to see musicals and visit museums. After I moved to Houston, my office was located right in the center of Houston's Theater District. After work, I often walked to a theater to see a performance, whether it was a Yo-Yo Ma concert or an opera *La Traviata.*

Most interests lead to hobbies which we pursue outside of work. Fleeting or staying, they always enrich our life and make life exciting. However, most of us spend the largest share of our days working. We want to be cautious about what I call a "bogus interest" before we commit to or invest in an interest as a career choice.

Be Careful with "Bogus Interests"

Interests can be inspired by many factors. Sometimes an interest is genuine and intrinsic. Sometimes it is extrinsic and meant to prove oneself, to impress others, or to follow the herd. The key difference between genuine interests and bogus interests is whether you feel the inner joy as you pursue the interest. We want to pursue a genuine interest when considering a career, rather than a bogus interest.

It's helpful to validate a career interest with these questions: Do I choose this interest because of my own intrinsic motivation, or do I simply copy it from someone else? Do I really feel joy in pursuing the interest, or is it more about impressing others? Am I truly interested in what's involved in the work or am I enamored by some perceived image?

I have had a lot of bogus interests in the past. After graduating from college, I thought I was interested in accounting. Several of my classmates went to work in the accounting department in the U.S. or European owned companies. At the time, accounting was considered as a decent career choice in China. There was also an allure about working in foreign companies because China had just opened the door to these companies. Although I was not genuinely interested in accounting work, I copied the interest from my classmates and I thought the choice would impress others too.

Commitment to a bogus interest would lead to disappointments and frustrations. My personality was seriously misaligned with accounting work. Although I learned a lot about the U.S. business culture from the job, the mechanical and repetitive side of accounting work quickly wore me out.

Passion: The Most Intense Interest

Of all the interests, passion offers us the deepest fulfillment in life. Passion can be viewed as an interest in its most intense form. Passion involves deep desire, intense drive and strong feelings of enthusiasm and excitement. It leads to the strongest devotion and commitment, which are crucial to overcome the many challenges on the way to realize a dream. There are several differences between passion and general interests.

First, a general interest only involves moderate emotions. It can be expressed as "I like it" or "I want to do it." But a passion is intensely emotional and involves strong enthusiasm, excitement and drive. It can be expressed as "I love it" or "I must do it." Second, a general interest only touches certain aspects of our lives, but a passion is something fundamental to one's fulfillment and something you don't want to live without. You constantly think about it and want to do it, be it, and have it. Third, a general interest may change from time to time, but a passion lasts a long time and most likely a lifetime. Passion may lead to a calling that you would like to pursue throughout your life.

You may be passionate about an activity, such as photography or dancing. You may be passionate about an opportunity, such as a business opportunity which may lead you to financial freedom. You may be passionate about a mission, such as creating education opportunities for children in underdeveloped countries. As you think about your passion, don't limit yourself and don't omit things that you feel are not important or special. It doesn't matter how others think of your passion as long as the passion is genuine for you.

If you are not clear about your passion, knowledge of your temperament, natural talents, values, dreams and preferred activities may point you to a unique and satisfying direction. Some of the organizations that specialize in temperament and aptitude research also offer tools to aid the discovery of interests, based on which you can further identify your passion. You may start by asking yourself the following questions:

- ❦ What are your temperament, natural talents and values? See next chapter for more information on values.
- ❦ What did you enjoy most in elementary school, middle school, high school, college?
- ❦ What activities excite you most after school, on weekends and during vacations?
- ❦ What topics do you like to talk about in conversations?
- ❦ What kind of friends do you like to hang out with?
- ❦ What kinds of books, magazines, websites, TV shows do you like to read, browse, watch?
- ❦ What would you like to do if you had enough time and money and did not have to make a living?
- ❦ What are some of your peak moments in life? What are the elements that make your peak moments?

During my self-discovery, I confirmed my passion in helping people grow and realize their potential, as well as my passion in living a life of health and freedom.

I discovered my other passion in singing through an unexpected opportunity. Sometimes love happens at the first sight, and sometimes it takes time for love to sparkle and grow. The same goes for passion. As you give yourself the opportunity to experiment in a wide variety of activities, your passion may discover you.

Both my daughters play musical instruments. I thought it would be nice if the three of us could make music together, which was only a vague idea until I met Dr. Dan (Vanessa) Liao, my music teacher. A distinguished soprano, Vanessa is the first Chinese woman artist, and one of the only five Asian artists so far, who have received a Ph.D. degree in Classic Vocal Performance. Before moving to the U.S., she performed in the prestigious opera houses across Europe and played leading roles in operas such as *Turandot, La Bohème* and *The Magic Flute*, to name a few.

Vanessa and I had an immediate personal connection. As I learned more about her, I was amazed that she had such an unusual and impressive professional background. Up to that point, it had never crossed my mind that someday I would learn Bel Canto singing. Even the word "Soprano" sounded dramatic and intimidating.

However, Vanessa's background inspired my interest in singing (again, you never know what could inspire an interest!) It also inspired my confidence. I knew I would learn great things from her, although I had no idea what I would learn. Now, with Vanessa's help, I have found my unique voice and have been able to make periodic breakthroughs in techniques. I also discovered a certain level of music aptitude in me, which enabled me to learn challenging songs in a relatively short time.

This interest has grown into a passion over time. I always enjoy practicing when my schedule allows. My children and I performed together on several occasions, just as I dreamed about. I genuinely have fallen in love with singing. It's the one hobby that I want to continue to pursue throughout my life.

Dust Off Your Childhood

As a critical part of finding your passion, I also strongly suggest that you dust off your childhood memories. A series of remarkable studies by British behavioral scientists over a twenty-eight-year period is very relevant here. The object of this exercise was to track childhood attitudes into adulthood.

In the first study, released several decades ago, a collection of seven-year-old children was interviewed in depth about their likes and dislikes, their outlooks and opinions, their vision of their personal futures. What did they most like doing? What did they want to do as grown-ups? The interviews were filmed and shown on the BBC as a TV documentary. That first study was entitled "Seven-Up." Seven years later, a documentary of new interviews with the same children—now adolescents—was called "14-Up." This was followed by "21-Up," "28-Up," and, later, "35-Up," when the subjects were well into adulthood.

This extensive study confirmed that what we love and do well as children continues to manifest itself as we become adults. Surprisingly, all the subjects eventually engaged in a profession or pursuit related to the interests they had had when they were age 7 to 14. Although most had strayed from those interests during adolescence and early adulthood—in some cases, going in entirely different directions—virtually all found their way back toward their childhood impulses, even if only in their hobbies, by the age of 35.

An excellent exercise is to spend a weekend with family members or friends, and dust off your childhood memories. Let yourself go. Remember what you really wanted to do as a child. You can enrich this process by checking the biographies of well-known adults whose passions began as children.

As a child in England, he spent hours and hours creating cardboard sets and elaborate staging for the puppet shows and miniature stage shows he would produce to entertain his family. Later in life, Andrew Lloyd Webber entertained the world with musicals including *Evita, Cats,* and *Phantom of the Opera.* At 14, she pondered a career in lawmaking while visiting state capitols during summer vacation. Sandra Day O'Connor became the first woman justice of the U.S. Supreme Court.

Ever since he was 12, he dreamed of doing something important in aviation. Neil Armstrong became the first person to walk on the moon. An awkward, nondescript girl in New York was totally obsessed with becoming a professional entertainer. She grew into Barbra Streisand. As a child, he loved woodworking and violin music. Antonio Stradivari became the world's most acclaimed violin maker.

As I dusted off my own childhood memories, it confirmed my passion for helping people grow and realize their potential. As a child, I relished everything from reading, writing, to storytelling and debating. Since middle school, I have always been interested in the subjects in humanities and social sciences. I dreamed of becoming someone who could help people through words and ideas, such as a journalist, an author, or a teacher.

As children, we had fantasies about what we wanted to be when we grew up—entertainer, scientist, world leader, astronaut, entrepreneur. We tried on numerous roles during our play-filled days of childhood and our dream-filled days of adolescence. Each role, job, or successful accomplishment seemed equally possible to us and equally real in our imaginations.

As we grew older, we began to narrow the possibilities. Some careers seemed beyond our reach. We were advised or ill-advised as the case might be that we couldn't be, shouldn't be, or wouldn't be successful.

Too often, our possibilities were narrowed by ourselves or by our choice to believe the limiting opinions of others, to the point where we began to live with a tightly compressed self-image. The vast fertile fields of our lives began to shrink from the image of a towering redwood tree in our mind's eye until we saw our future plot of success as being a "flowerpot" in size. Suddenly, in our imaginations, most of the world seemed impossible or inaccessible to us.

The critical point to recognize is that both the unlimited potential of childhood and the tight constraints of adulthood originate and reside primarily in the imagination. What we imagine is what we become.

Like many people, I landed on a career path that was disconnected from my childhood passions and dreams. I had enough talents to be competent at my jobs. It was not the sweetest zone but it was a comfort zone. My self-discovery gave me the courage to step beyond my comfort zone and explore my true passion. If you happen to be in such a comfort zone, I also encourage you to courageously explore your true passion.

Regardless of where each of us is in our quest for fulfillment, never let your first job determine your life from there ever after. Nor should we let others, or money alone, dominate our long-range decisions. We must take the first step toward a life strategy by being true to ourselves.

Most Telling Predictor of Greatness

Passion, the inner drive for excellence, motivates you to be the best you possibly can in whatever you do. As leaders or parents, you want to be careful not to overly emphasize external motivators—money, perks, travels and titles—in trying to motivate your team members or children. Enduring motivation comes ultimately from within the individual.

Behavioral scientists have found that independent desire for excellence is the most telling predictor of significant achievement. In other words, the success of our efforts depends less on the efforts themselves than on our motives. The most successful people, in almost all fields, have achieved their greatness out of a desire to express what they felt had to be expressed.

Often it was a desire to use their talents and abilities to the utmost. This is not to say that many of them did not also reap financial rewards. Many of them did, and some of the wealthiest individuals in the world have converted their passions and natural gifts into a fortune. But far more than thoughts of profit, the key to their success was the inspiration and the flame of passion burning within.

Vanessa: A Life Driven by Passion

Vanessa is my music teacher as well as my dear friend. I resonate deeply with her passionate, intuitive personality, her impeccable taste in music, art and style, and her genuine appreciation of all that is truly beautiful. Her life stories, richly reflecting passion and perseverance, are constant inspirations to me.

Her singing talent was recognized when she was a child. When she heard a song played on the radio, she could immediately learn it and sing it. Born into a highly-educated family in China, with mom as a doctor and dad as a professor, she was expected to pursue a traditional academic path. However, because she always sang as she walked in the neighborhood, several neighbors noticed her unusual musicality and her beautiful voice. They suggested to her parents that they should find ways to help her develop her singing talent.

She started music training as an elementary school student. At age fifteen, she was admitted into a special music high school associated with Sichuan Conservatory of Music. She had been chosen as the only vocal student out of thousands of candidates in southwest China. This marked the formal beginning of her music career. Several years later, she was selected to attend Shanghai Conservatory of Music—one of the best music institutes in China—which recruited only ten vocal students a year out of the numerous candidates competing across the country.

These accomplishments were more than impressive to any outsider's eyes, however, life was never as glamorous as it appeared on the surface. She later learned that luck played a role when she was selected into the music college. Although she didn't sing as well as her classmates, the judges saw her potential to develop into a great opera singer, a type of talent that was lacking in China at the time.

Unfortunately, that potential didn't become a reality. She was highly intelligent and excelled in all other academic areas, but continued to fall behind in her vocal performance, the single most important measure for a vocal student. The music world was cruelly competitive. Her early confidence was peeled away, layer by layer. College graduation could have marked the end of her dream to become a world class singer. She could have chosen to leave the painful memories behind, accept her status as a mediocre singer or possibly go on to become a mediocre music teacher.

One day, however, Vanessa informed her parents that she planned to go to Europe to pursue a singing career. Knowing what she had gone through, her parents were shocked and torn between discouraging her and encouraging her choice. They were very concerned that this decision would even further damage their daughter's self-esteem. However, they eventually supported her to pursue her passion.

As a parent, I know how agonizingly they must have struggled. I have great respect for parents like them, who show a tremendous amount of courage in dealing with their children's difficult decisions. In spite of their apprehension, they understand that a worthwhile life is often about taking a leap of faith and moving forward into unchartered territories.

As Vanessa has often said, "God always directs the way for an eagerly seeking heart." At her very first lesson in Finland, she was told that she was born to be a soprano! It was a stark awakening, since during all of her former academic training, she had been taught as a mezzo-soprano. She finally understood what had gone wrong and why she hadn't progressed as she had expected. It was a bittersweet moment. She felt a renewed sense of hope, yet also recognized that, once again, she was at a new starting point.

After a brief stay in Finland, she went on to The Hochschule für Musik Nürnberg, a music conservatory in Germany, to pursue her Ph.D. education. She had to learn German in addition to learning to become a soprano. There were months and months of hard work. Gradually, as it was when she was a child, everyone around her was impressed by how well she sang.

However, being completely self-honest, she knew there was a gap between where she was and the road to the world-class stage. She went to Italy, reaching out to several masters and hoping to become their student. Unfortunately, she received a "no" from all of them, some politely and some bluntly. Once again, she demonstrated resilience, an important quality to survive in the music world of incredible subjectivity.

Through an unexpected sequence of events, she met Grace Bumbry, a world-renowned opera singer and receiver of 2009 Kennedy Center Honors. Mrs. Bumbry saw her potential and took her on as a student. The three years' training with Mrs. Bumbry was extremely tough yet worth all the tears and sweat. Not only were her techniques and style perfected, her taste for music was elevated to a new height.

After more than fifteen years of persistent pursuit, she saw herself finally reach the point of becoming a world class singer. The ugly duckling crying in the college dorm finally transformed into her true self, a beautiful swan. As a Chinese soprano, she performed in leading roles at major opera houses in Europe, a remarkable accomplishment in a highly competitive field dominated by singers from the western world.

When we had dinner together recently, I asked Vanessa, "What motivated you to persevere for so many years? Was it the dream to sing on the world class opera stage?" She said, "I was so curious about how the masters could sing like that. I really, really wanted to figure it out. If they could do it, I knew I could do it. I honestly didn't think much about specific goals, such as status or money." Her husband Tao was with us at that dinner. He is a brilliant tenor and a rising star on the international opera stage. Tao echoed her sentiments, "Music is pure, beautiful and magic. You are hooked once you get into it."

Today Vanessa and Tao are continuing to pursue their passion in music. As a close friend to both of them, I see the same level of passion in their new endeavors. It's the pure passion and desire for excellence that have driven them and so many people to persevere in the journey to achieve their dreams.

Which Path Will Your Passion Follow?

For Vanessa and Tao, their passion in music has led them to a professional path. Although I am also passionate about singing, I have treated it as a hobby with no intention to turn it into a career. As we explore our passions, we may fall in love with something that ignites the sparkles in our hearts. As some point, it may lead to the next big question: will it be a non-profitable passion expressed as hobby or volunteer work, or a profitable passion that can turn into a career or a business?

To discern between these two types of passions, we want to ask ourselves a few realistic questions: Who would benefit from our passion? Who would be willing to pay for our passion? How large is the market and demand? How competitive is the field? What could we do to make it happen? Furthermore, would we really want to pursue it as a career? For some people, a passion is just for fun. Turning it into a business could sacrifice some of the fun, as it could become a "have to do" with financial pressures.

My passion for singing has been purely a hobby. I can polish my skills and enjoy the entire process personally, but I know how competitive the music world is. At this point, I am very much aware of the difference between my current voice and what I would refer to as a professional voice. I don't expect people to rave about my performance to a point where they are willing to pay for it. My family and friends may come to hear me sing, if I offer them free tickets. Others most likely wouldn't come even if the tickets are free!

As with many things in life, there needs to be a healthy balance of idealism and realism. As much as we want to "follow our hearts," we want to be realistic about what it takes to develop a passion into a career or a business.

My passion in helping others grow has potential for development into a future career. I can figure out a direction and build my skills to move toward that goal. Many people express their passion through volunteering or freelancing before turning the passion into a main career or business. It's never too late to rekindle our dreams and to pursue a new calling.

Ingredient for a Wonderful Life

The passion of pursuit seems to be one of the ingredients for a long, healthy and joyful life. Never to have had a passion and ever to have fully depleted your passion can be two of life's greatest tragedies. Pursuit of a passion wears out very few people. But people rust out by the hundreds of thousands when they lose the fire in their heart.

On the morning television *Today Show* some time ago, the host interviewed a Mr. Smith, who was celebrating his 102nd birthday. Mr. Smith had brought along his favorite potted plants. The host became a bit annoyed when Mr. Smith's fond attention was focused on his chrysanthemums and orchids.

"But Mr. Smith, we'd all like to know to what you attribute your long life?" the host asked, saying they only had a minute remaining. Mr. Smith, not the least senile, continued showing off his flowers. He touched them, sprayed them with water, and gazed at them affectionately—while the clock ticked on at $100,000 per minute. "This little lovely won't bloom for another two years," he chuckled. The TV host made a final attempt in the few seconds remaining to discover the guest's formula for longevity: "What's your secret for living so long and staying so excited?"

The old man replied with a question of his own: "Who would take care of my flowers?" The host sighed and the director cut away to a commercial. Had the viewers understood Mr. Smith's very profound point? He might never see some of his flowers in full bloom, but he had just given millions one of the secrets of longevity: have a purpose that will outlive you and pursue it with passion.

7

Values: The Guiding Lights

It's not hard to make decisions,
when you know what your values are.
—*Roy Disney*

Values are the beliefs, principles and preferences that form our inner compass. If we can articulate our values, we are more likely to establish goals and make decisions in a way that is coherent and genuinely fulfilling to us. For a girl born with a talent and a passion for dancing, she may be most fulfilled by becoming a dance teacher if she values family and children; or she may be most fulfilled by becoming a professional dancer if she values social recognition and exciting life experiences.

Core values are probably some of the most overlooked traits, but it is critical to clarify our values in order to live in a way that is in harmony with our inner self. Most of us have a vague sense of our values, which influence our choices to varying degrees. However, only a few of us take the time to articulate our values and use them to consciously and consistently guide our lives. As a result, we make impulsive decisions which may cause frustrations or regrets later on, like going to new places without a map.

Many people, in pursuit of money, choose a career or a business that is in direct conflict with their values. One who values kindness and respect joins a high-pressure firm where rudeness and profanities are the norm. One who values family life finds himself locked into a noon to midnight restaurant business, leaving him with virtually no time to spend with his wife and children.

Others, out of initial attraction, marry someone with few values in common. One partner values family and considers children as the most essential part of life; while the other values personal enjoyment and thinks that children would disrupt their life. One partner values experiential living; while the other derives satisfaction in material possessions. There are few life challenges greater than living with or working with others whose values are in conflict with our own.

Discover Your Values

Each of us may hold different values, which are influenced by our family, friends, life experiences, religious beliefs, and of course, our personal uniqueness. Some values are our beliefs such as our faith, our world view or personal philosophies. Some values are the core principles by which we live, such as kindness, gratitude and respect. Some values are more about our priorities or preferences in life, such as security vs. adventure.

When we talk about values, we often refer to beliefs and principles. However, it's equally important to clarify our priorities and preferences in order to live a truly fulfilling life. I followed this process to get clarity on my own priorities and preferences.

I started with building my value vocabulary. You can find a long list of common values by searching "values" or "value list" online. You may also want to review studies on universal values led by Psychologist S. H. Schwartz. A value is a universal value if it has the same value or worth for almost all people. The study included surveys of more than 25,000 people in 44 countries with a wide range of different cultural types, and led to ten types of universal values, such as power, achievement, and security; as well as fifty-six specific universal values under the ten types.

You can find these universal values online. Out of the many values people could possibly live by, you want to identify the values that matter most to you as an individual, and rank them in the order of importance to you.

For a more methodical approach, you can complete Rokeach Value Survey (RVS). Developed by social psychologist Milton Rokeach. The instrument is designed to help you rank the 36 values, including 18 terminal values and 18 instrumental values, based on their importance to you. Terminal Values refer to the goals that a person would like to achieve in life, such as freedom, social recognition, and family security. Instrumental Values refer to the preferable behaviors, such as responsible, honest, and loyal. Reflect on these values and circle those most applicable to you.

As you reflect on the values that matter most to you in life, these questions may be helpful to you:

- What are the happiest and most fulfilling moments and events in your life?
- When are the most frustrating, depressing, and regretful moments, events in your life?
- What has given you the most pride in yourself?
- What kind of lifestyle would you enjoy most?
- Who are the people you care for the most?
- Who are the people you admire most? What makes you admire them?
- For the values important to you, how and why do they become important to you?
- Do you live by these important values now? Why and why not?

As a result of my values discovery, I identified my priorities and preferences as: family, friendship, health, freedom, helping others, self-actualization, and rich life experiences.

Follow What's Truly Important to You

Before we commit to a set of values, whether they are beliefs, principles or preferences, it's important to consider the factors that may influence our values. Some values are fundamental principles or virtues to most if not all humanity, such as honesty, integrity and respect. We always want to cultivate these values, for our own good and for the good of the society. Other values are matters of personal philosophies or preferences. There is no absolute right or wrong, better or worse about them. For these types of values, we sometimes can become confused about our values when we adopt other people's values as our own.

Let's say your parents greatly value financial security, but you are willing to sacrifice financial security for adventure. Will you adopt your parents' values, perhaps following their career and lifestyle suggestions, or will you become your own self? You may feel that your values don't match some that are fundamental to your parents. We all face that possibility. Always remember that your values are those significantly important to you, not necessarily to others.

Sometimes people's dreams are suffocated by their family or friends with different values. A woman who values professional achievement may feel guilty to pursue her dream if her husband believes that a woman's role is to stay home and take care of housework. You may not be able to change other people's values, but you can influence them by your example, especially the people you love the most. You also can choose to surround yourself with people who share similar values and can support you during happy or trying times.

Unlearn Old Values and Embrace New Values

I had to "unlearn" some of the values influenced by my environment, before I embraced the values genuinely important to me, such as my personal philosophies about work, job security and money.

Work Is Unpleasant or Is It?

Based on the statistics provided by the U.S. Department of Labor, for people employed between ages 25 to 54, the average time spent at work is 8.9 hours a day, which accounts for the largest period of time out of the 24 hours a day; sleeping comes in second with an average of 7.7 hours a day. Over the course of a lifetime, most of us will have spent over 80,000 hours at work. Obviously, work has a tremendous impact on our happiness.

However, based on global research conducted by Gallup, with national representatives from more than 140 countries, only 13% of people worldwide actually like going to work, and are "engaged" in their work. 63% of people are "not engaged" or simply unmotivated. The remaining 24% are "actively disengaged" or truly unhappy. Looking at this depressing data, it's no surprise why it is such a commonly held notion that "work is by nature not pleasant," or, "I have to do things I don't enjoy to make a living."

My acceptance of the idea "work is by nature unpleasant" was rooted in my early school years. As students, we faced fierce competition at every school age because the college seats in China were very limited when I was growing up. To have a chance to enter a good college, it was important to get into a top high school, a top middle school and even a top elementary school.

It was a situation described as "thousands of soldiers crossing a single wood bridge." Most little soldiers would fall off the bridge somewhere along the way. Only a small group could make it to the other end of the bridge, the final station called college.

I formally joined the "thousands of soldiers" beginning in middle school. Study was a 7am-9pm duty that I must perform. Being a good student, I strived to do my best in everything I was required to do. Of course, there were unpleasant feelings such as boredom, anxiety, and low motivation. However, I accepted the notion that I needed to live with these feelings in order to have a better life. This belief that work and joy were incompatible continued, and became ingrained in my subconscious, even as I entered the work force.

Many of us accept negative feelings as normal once the feelings become routine or habitual. We get used to this so-called drudgery, although we continue to feel unhappy, unfulfilled or even unhealthy. Some people live in a chronic sub-health condition, with low energy, fatigue and other symptoms. However, they become accustomed to it after a period of time. Because they lose touch with how it feels to be truly healthy, they are not eager to improve the situation as they could and should.

These negative habitual patterns, undetected and hidden deeply beneath our consciousness, can powerfully hinder our fulfillment in life. As I became aware of my own hidden beliefs and habitual forces during self-discovery, I began to question them and open my mind to new perspectives and beliefs.

Amazingly, I started to encounter people who would reinforce these new beliefs. After recognizing that "work can be pleasant and joyful," I have met many people who found their calling, enjoyed their work and made a good living. They are individuals in a variety of professions, including corporate executives, business owners, teachers, interpreters and musicians.

One of these individuals is Mrs. Guest, my daughters' elementary school music teacher. Mrs. Guest has been a music teacher for more than twenty years. My daughters love her child-friendly expression, and enjoy the beautiful songs she teaches in class and in choir. In one of our school concerts, Mrs. Guest shared this with parents and students, "Students always come to me and ask why I wanted to be a music teacher. It was because I love children and I love music. To me, work is play. What can be happier than every day coming to work for play?"

I resonated deeply with this simple, straightforward statement. "Wow," I thought to myself, "This is exactly what I want!"

Job Security or Freedom of Choice?

Just as I had completely changed my attitude from "work is an unpleasant necessity" to the internalized concept of viewing work as play, I also changed my attitude toward job security.

For most people in my generation, the ideal path of life was to study hard, go to a good college, get a secure job and work until we retire. Even today, job security is still a value that many parents are trying to instill in their children. I considered job security as my key value until I was awakened by realities.

I used to work for a giant, global corporation back in China. At the time, it was one of the most admired companies in the U.S., offering excellent salaries, generous benefits and upward mobility. I was very proud to be an employee there. Coincidentally, ten years later, I moved to Illinois and worked in its headquarter office, as a finance manager for one of its contracting companies.

I was stunned to witness the company's massive layoffs and continual downsizing due to its drastically reduced market share and earnings. This experience was a resounding wake-up call for me. It was eye opening to realize that companies today can go from "sunrise" into "sunset" status very rapidly with economic environment changes, and as technological breakthroughs create sudden obsolescence. The notion of "job security" had become an oxymoron like "skin deep," "good grief" and "growing smaller."

Later on, there came another awakening moment. After I had my second child, I experienced chronic fatigue due to years of juggling work, children, and school. My chronic fatigue was compounded by the most severe stress I had ever experienced at work. At that time, I happened to be in the project manager role which was seriously misaligned with my temperament, as mentioned earlier in the book.

With my new responsibilities as a parent, I began to develop an acute, painful feeling that financially—if I would like to offer my children the best possible opportunities—I would be bound to a 9-5 job from then on, whether I liked it or not. Suddenly, I became one of the people mostly dependent upon outside forces. Intrinsically, I was still that free-spirited child. The fear of losing freedom of choice was suffocating to me.

Many people, like me, experience deep frustrations at some point in their careers. The frustrations may be triggered by the changes in their own life situations, such as new family responsibilities, or becoming less competitive in the market place as they get older. The frustrations may also be triggered by their office environment, such as monotonous work, stressed relationships with bosses or coworkers, or resentment over the promotion they deserve but never receive. There seems to be one dominating root cause for the frustrations: the lack of freedom of choice.

I began to observe those individuals who had achieved freedom of choice and determined that there were three important paths to that destination.

The first path is to discover our true self and to express our true self through what we do, as discussed throughout this book, so that we can become a living example of viewing work as play. Most people today, unfortunately, go to work for the pay, not viewing work as play.

The second path is to become financially free. Being financially free means being able to generate enough residual income—from business, investment, network, or other forms of assets—to provide us and our family the standard of living we choose, without having to depend on day to day work.

Financial freedom offers the time freedom with which we can pursue our other passions, such as hobbies, travels, charity work or community services, without worrying about our livelihood. It affords us the possibility of retiring young or retiring early.

"Being financially free" is distinctly different from "appearing rich." You may seem rich—with a $400,000 annual income, a 5,000 sq. ft. house and luxury cars; but you are not financially free if you must continue to work to sustain your standard of living. You may not appear rich—with only $100,000 annual income, a comfortable, modest house and an economical car; but you are financially free if you don't have to work day to day to sustain your standard of living.

It's the source of our income—where our income will come from when we no longer want to work or are capable of working—that fundamentally determines whether we can be financially free.

What distinguishes those who achieve financial freedom are primarily their mindset and the choices they make, not necessarily how much harder or longer they work. Again, everyone has a maximum of 24 hours a day, without exception.

To become financially free and potentially retire early, they usually make a deliberate choice of building income-generating assets, in whatever form they may choose, supported by financial discipline and an entrepreneurial mindset.

With the mindset of trading hours for dollars—which is the case for many employed or self-employed individuals—it is extremely difficult to accomplish this goal. For many of us, it's already challenging to retire at what is considered as the normal retirement age, after a long and industrious career, with our savings.

Although it is preferable, you don't have to love what you do to become financially free. What you should be passionate about is the opportunity—the opportunity to fulfill your dream and build a future worthy of your inner applause. Not all entrepreneurs are born to love sales pitches and rejections. They persist in pursuing leads and doing the follow-ups anyway, because they love the opportunities that will result from perseverance.

The third path to reach freedom of choice, of course, is the most ideal which is to integrate the first path and the second path into one magnificent road—reach financial freedom while working as play.

Freedom of choice, in many ways, represents "true security" and "true wealth." Whether you reach it through your passion for an activity, or your passion for an opportunity, you are taking what I refer to as "the road less traveled."

Real Value of Money

Although this is not meant to be a personal finance book, I encourage you to reflect on your attitude toward money as part of your values discovery. Whether we want to face it or not, money is a necessity upon which we all depend, and it impacts many aspects of our lives.

I had a traditional Chinese upbringing, which valued academic and intellectual achievement more than anything else. As part of my early experience, I acquired the notion that it was in poor taste and even a sign of greediness to talk about money and think about money, especially for people with higher educations.

The most honorable path in life, as mentioned earlier, was to enter a top college and acquire a secure job—affording a modest, comfortable lifestyle—with money forever staying in the background. That was exactly what I did. It wasn't until my self-discovery that I began to reflect on my own attitude toward money.

Throughout history, a prevailing mindset has been that money is the root of all evils. Some people, like the old me, hold a disdain for money because money is a vulgar subject to them. Some people despise money, because to get it, a necessary evil, they have to work doing something they don't like. Some people are oppressed by money, because they are dependent on its sources.

Of course, many people are greedy for money because money gives them the appearance of being powerful and superior. Private jets, yachts, magnificent estates and luxurious leisure bombard people's senses to the point where "Get-rich-quick-schemes" seduce people into wishful thinking about getting the most, the soonest, by doing the least. Some venture to get rich through illegal or unethical activities and enterprises.

In spite of the negatives associated with money, it is the greed for money, not money itself, that is one of the roots of evil. Just as fire can cook food and can also burn people, money can be the fuel for both good and evil purposes. It all depends on how it is acquired and utilized. When money is acquired legally and ethically, as well as employed wisely and prudently, it is a positive force that empowers people and enhances life.

Money is a foundation for the basic level of living and fulfillment. Across the world, due to lack of financial resources, so many children have been denied the education they deserve, so many talented individuals have given up on developing their talents and pursuing their dreams, and so many millions of families have no way out of a life of poverty and disease.

Money provides you freedom and independence. It releases you from the petty problems and tyranny of the small issues in life, like car problems, home repairs, and so forth. It helps you live your life without as much fear of catastrophic loss. You can risk pursuing your dreams more. It gives you more control over your daily life. You can go where and when you want, and pay your bills as you go.

Money gives you dignity and security in your senior years. Most people live the so-called golden years in near-poverty, depending on state and federal agencies, or their relatives, for their survival needs. Retirement, for most people, means being cast aside and no longer relevant. The problem is, because of medical intervention, we are living a lot longer than we can afford to, and the quality of life doesn't usually match the quantity.

Money enables you to support causes you believe in, in a material way, and can be distributed to those who need and deserve your help. It can help you become a stronger influence for the good in the world. Money isn't just for toys and gadgets. It's for building factories, highways, research centers, hospitals, laboratories, and youth centers. It helps feed hungry children in underdeveloped nations and neighborhoods.

Sadly, 80% of the humans on earth are poor, living on less than $10 a day. The majority of them are desperately poor. Success to any member of such a family is to have some land to till and a way to provide nourishment for the children so that they are able to survive into adulthood. Money, from philanthropists and charities, can make a life and death difference for the underprivileged people.

Money, when earned through honest work and dedication, is concrete evidence of accomplishment and builds the character of personal achievement, self-respect and responsibility. When ordinary people, against all odds, become self-sufficient or financially free, they are often driven by responsibilities or dreams beyond materialism, such as offering their children the best future. Their stories are sources of inspiration.

To me, money is not a destination, but a vehicle. It is a vehicle that affords us the freedom of expressing who we are; a vehicle to fulfill our responsibilities in life; and a vehicle for us to do greater good for the world.

Beyond basic necessities to survive, each of us has a different interest level concerning money and different abilities in making money. No matter where we are on the scale, it's our attitude and motivation that count.

Many of the greatest people throughout history have lived with only the most basic material necessities. Because they passionately lived their calling, money was simply fuel for their journey. However, a disdain for money, as I once held, is an entirely different attitude. It's not necessarily an indicator of moral or intellectual superiority as I had thought.

Sometimes the attitude becomes an excuse for people to avoid challenges and hard work, to a point where they can't fulfill basic responsibilities in life. Sometimes the attitude becomes an obstacle which prevents people from realizing their potential. A man said to an accomplished entrepreneur, "I want to be an entrepreneur, but I am not comfortable about the idea of *making money*." The entrepreneur responded thoughtfully, "Go ahead and make money; then give it away to charities, as I did."

Too often we care so much about "appearing" noble that we forget what it truly means to be noble. Even for the believers in God, some are more concerned about how they appear in others' eyes than how they can truly help people and honor God.

With money, as with everything else in life, we want to always examine our attitude and motivation.

Wisdom Behind Blessings

If holding a disdain for money is like living with an invisible barrier, being intoxicated by the power of money is like living in a mirage. There is the law of diminishing marginal utility—simply put, the first piece of steak tastes like heaven for a hungry man, but the pleasure becomes less and less, and may even turn into displeasure, as the man devours more pieces of steak. Similarly, money—from zero up to a certain point—can increase happiness significantly. Beyond this point, the happiness that it brings gradually diminishes, and without wisdom, may even turn negative.

As a child, I enjoyed simple pleasures immensely, some of which, surprisingly, were blessings of material scarcity. When I was seven years old, a family friend who worked in the south China brought us some bananas. It was my first time to see a banana. My brother and I only dared to take tiny bites, afraid that it would be gone too fast. The banana tasted incredibly smooth and yummy—a taste that I have never found the same.

As part of the Chinese New Year tradition, everyone would wear a new outfit for the New Year's day. My grandma usually hand-made the new clothes for my brother and me. Our excitement started to build up even as we watched her making them. Once she put the finished clothes in the drawer, we would secretly open the drawer and check on them every day.

As material abundance increased, however, I found myself less sensitive about simple pleasures and less able to feel happy. I also found that the excitement resulting from material acquisitions, and even personal achievements, was only short and fleeting.

Studies have suggested that depression is more common in wealthy countries than in the less wealthy and less industrialized ones. Given my own experience, I am not surprised by the finding. I had never heard of the term "depression" when I lived in China more than twenty years ago. However, with the booming economy, depression affects more and more Chinese as it has affected Americans.

Fortunately, I was able to re-connect with the simple pleasures and re-cultivate my ability to feel happy as I learned to live with purpose and simplicity.

Ancient Chinese philosophy emphasizes that in order to be truly blessed, people must have the level of wisdom that matches the level of what they are given, whether it is money, fame or even physical beauty.

One aspect of this wisdom involves the self-discipline of living with simplicity and higher purpose even as the level of riches increases. The billionaires who live a very simple life but relentlessly give back to society, such as Mark Zuckerberg, founder of Facebook, exemplify this type of wisdom. Without self-discipline, greater riches could lead to greater trouble. This is not an unusual phenomenon in big prize lottery winners and inheritors of large estates who are not prepared to handle their fortunes.

Another aspect of this wisdom involves not being trapped by material possessions. Ancient Chinese described one of the tragedies in life as people being enslaved by material possessions. Many of us enjoy only a small percentage of our belongings, but have to spend hours and hours in handling clutters or maintaining the things that we rarely use. In a way, I am glad that I don't have a finished basement, which forces my family to keep less stuff.

My aspiration for a life of freedom led me to embrace the concept of minimalist living. For me, minimalist living goes beyond thrifty living. It's a matter of precision— precision about what we truly need and what we truly enjoy, rooted in deep self-knowledge. You could have a minimum number of items, but items with the finest quality, beauty and elegance. The principle of minimalist living can be applied to every aspect of our lives—from food, material belongings, to social activities and relationships.

Minimalist living enhances our ability to feel happiness as well as our sensitivity to simple pleasures, because it frees the mind, heart and spirit, giving space to what's truly essential in life.

A beautiful life, to me, involves a minimum number of material belongings that are just enough to nurture the soul but never burden it; a rich amount of beautiful, fascinating, inspiring experiences; the abundant freedom to pursue passions, fulfill responsibilities and help others; and most importantly, loving relationships with family, friends and a personal connection with God, the ultimate source of wisdom.

Our values, collectively, form our inner compass and our unique definition of success. As I pursue my own definition of success, I hope you too will identify and cultivate the values most conducive to your happiness and well-being, think and act congruently according to these values and become successful, according to your own definition.

8

Taking the Road Less Travelled

I shall be telling this with a sigh Somewhere ages and ages
hence:
Two roads diverged in a wood, and I—
I took the one less traveled by,
And that has made all the difference.
— *Robert Frost*

As I discovered my temperament, natural talents, passions and values, I felt as if God made a beautiful sketch of me even before I was born. However, along the way, I lost that sketch and began to paint following other sketches. I was so excited to re-discover my own sketch, and I couldn't wait to design my life accordingly.

Although I intuitively sensed my calling, it was through my self-discovery that I confirmed it and was motivated to make it a reality. As mentioned earlier, I have an "Idealist" temperament, which is characterized by a passionate concern for the growth and development of myself and others. I have identified my top five talent themes as connectedness, empathy, maximizer, intellection, and futuristic. My temperament and strengths are aligned with my passion which is to help people grow and achieve their potential. My childhood dreams are also well aligned with this passion.

This overall theme runs consistently across the various dimensions. You may also find in your self-discovery that the different dimensions about you are intricately connected, because each of us is a unique and holistic being.

Once we recognize our calling, we can get more specific on the direction we want to take, based on our values and personal philosophies. It is helpful to put together a detailed profile to reflect that specific direction. As a constant reminder, we can also make a dream board, a visual representation of our goals and dreams. My specific direction can be expressed as follows:

"My calling is to help people grow and achieve their potential as unique individuals. I want to see people become the best version of themselves, physically, mentally and spiritually. I will blend this calling into all areas of my life, through formal opportunities such as speaking, writing, teaching, coaching, or through casual conversations and interactions in everyday life.

My ideal work will involve rich, diverse, global experiences, and will allow flexibility and balance between work and family. I will make amazing connections with people of different backgrounds and touch their lives in meaningful ways. We will share many beautiful, sparkling and heartwarming moments together."

We can fulfill our calling through many possible choices and pathways. In today's rapidly changing world, there is rarely one perfect, clearly paved path. What matters is where and how we can offer the most value to others and to society utilizing our unique, authentic competencies. We want to remain nimble, open-minded and sensitive to the happenings and opportunities around us as we pursue our calling.

The Future "Career"

We are living in a fluid, fast forward and technology-driven world, a world in which careers and lifestyles will be constantly redefined. Across many industries, robots, artificial intelligence, and other new technologies have been changing the landscape of human careers.

Robots in manufacturing, medical, and a variety of office or home service fields are eliminating the need for many skilled and unskilled workers, because of the precision, reliability and economy offered. In Dubai, flying drone taxis already are in regular operation from the airport to solve the prime time driving traffic gridlock. Also, in Dubai, there are functioning "robocops"—robotic police officers on patrol. By 2030, Dubai is planning to have 25% of its police force manned by "robocops."

Computers and machines, equipped with artificial intelligence, are now capable of offering a wide range of sophisticated services, from translation to legal and medical consultation, with a higher quality and at a lower cost. In a test against three expert human radiologists, a technology based medical diagnoses solution was 50% better in classifying malignant tumors with a false negative rate of zero, compared with a false negative rate of 7% for the human doctors.

The list goes on and on: virtual reality, 3D printing, 4D printing... It's possible that more advanced technologies will have emerged by the time you read this book.

Two Oxford researchers, Carl Benedikt Frey and Michael A Osborn, analyzed the skills required for more than 700 occupations and concluded that machines are likely to take over 47% of today's jobs in a few decades.

As old careers fade and new careers are created in what seems to be the blink of an eye, we can no longer think of "career" or "job" as having one steady profession or one secure position. According to a survey conducted by Oxford Economics and SAP, over 83% of executives being surveyed plan on increasing their use of contingent, part-time, or flexible workers with in-demand skills. These workers will be hired to accomplish a specific project rather than given a full-time position.

Instead of "a paid position of regular employment," the future job will most likely fit better into its second definition in the dictionary, "a task or piece of work, especially one that is paid."

It is wise to look at the upside as well as the downside caused by these changes, as offered in a Chinese proverb "In every crisis, there is opportunity." Technologies are liberating people from repetitive, programmable work, and creating new, exciting career possibilities.

The future careers are likely to be more creative, more fun, more flexible and more human oriented. Work and life may blend and overlap. Freelancing, home-based businesses and services that are creative, unique and unconventional are likely to become increasingly popular.

The future is about differentiation and personalization. During marketing classes about ten years ago, we were talking about market segmentation—differentiating products, services and information to tailor them to the needs and interests of a segmented group. Now we talk about personalization—differentiating everything to a point that it is tailored to the needs and interests of each individual. We are rapidly moving from "mass marketing" to "me marketing."

The same trend applies to marketing ourselves. In a world where we have to compete with robots and machines, it is no longer enough to offer generic, programmable, easy-to-duplicate skills. We need to offer a much stronger value to whomever we serve—clients, employers, audiences—by differentiating ourselves with our unique, authentic, hard-to-duplicate human competencies.

A successful business differentiation strategy is rooted in a deep understanding of the business's unique positions and its competitive environment, commonly referred as its SWOT (Strengths, Weakness, Opportunities, Threats). Similarly, a successful personal differentiation strategy should also be rooted in a deep understanding of the individual's unique SWOT.

In essence, this is a book about differentiation and personalization. By differentiating and personalizing our work and life choices according to who we are, we will not only live a joyful and fulfilling life, but also gain a powerful winning edge to succeed in the future world.

Stay True to Core Beliefs

To pursue our calling is exciting but challenging. We will face distractions and setbacks. A clear vision, a strong faith, and a commitment to consistently take actions are all critical in order not to be derailed off track or withdraw to our old paths.

After graduating from my MBA program, I was asked from time to time, "Why are you still at the same place?" Most of my classmates had moved on to a more promising career. I was not ready for change because Brooke was just a toddler. Nonetheless, propelled by the peer pressure, I sent out a few resumes for advancement opportunities within my profession. I was soon contacted by several companies and recruiters. One opportunity offered a potential 30-40% raise with broader responsibilities.

I was already on the self-discovery journey at that point and roughly knew what I wanted to do. However, the new direction seemed challenging and intimidating. I was clueless on how to bridge myself from where I was to where I wanted to be. Once again, I felt the familiar temptation to withdraw to my old easy path. I went for the phone interview. However, I started to feel uneasy when it was time for a face-to-face interview. After re-focusing on my dreams and my values, I declined the interview opportunity.

A vertical career advancement is still the dream for many corporate professionals, even as the world is changing and the term "career" is being redefined. However, I realized that at my stage of life, a big raise or a bigger title was not going to fundamentally change my life. More importantly, if I were to take on this opportunity, which was not aligned with my calling, it would completely derail me from pursuing my dreams.

As the noises quieted down, I was able to objectively evaluate my situation. At my gut level, I was happy where I was. Thankfully, I was no longer in that project manager role!

My company was a mission driven organization with more than a hundred years of history. In spite of the changes to keep up with the world, there was a strong sense of mission and a friendly atmosphere. Many employees had been there for a long time and were wonderful to work with. In my particular role, I enjoyed working with the teams I supported. They were intelligent, kind and fun. My boss was great to work with as well. She trusted the team members to work independently yet always offered support and coaching when necessary. My work was also well aligned with my analytical aptitude.

Considering these positive factors and my family situation, I didn't feel it was the right timing for a dramatic change. I recognized that in order to pursue my passion, I must develop my public speaking skills. I decided to take the first step toward realizing my calling—to join my company's Toastmasters Club.

Risk Being a Fool in the Eyes of Others

Much has been said about the fear of public speaking. As comedian Jerry Seinfeld humored, "...to the average person, if you go to a funeral, you're better off in the casket than doing the eulogy." For me, the fear was real, and stressful.

Although I was comfortable giving presentations at work, speaking publicly to an unfamiliar audience was a little intimidating. During my first speech, I was so nervous that I forgot what I had written about a minute into the talk. I plunged forward, but honestly didn't know what I was saying.

I was so thankful for my caring and supportive club members. It felt like they were using a magnifying glass to find everything positive to say about my disastrous, first attempt. I was embarrassed but, with their encouragement, I decided to keep going.

Getting out of my comfort zone, during my first attempt at public speaking, produced an important tip I want to pass on to you. To pursue a new calling requires building new skills. Some skills are easier and faster for you to acquire if they are aligned with your aptitudes. It may feel like something natural and enjoyable instead of hard labor. A gifted artist delights herself in learning new art techniques. A born-to-be engineer gets himself fully absorbed in the objects he engineers.

However, in many cases, you must move out of your comfort zone in order to build new skills, and you must risk looking and feeling foolish in the eyes of others. Across many professions or businesses, you must build a series of soft skills in order to be successful, including the skill of handling failures and setbacks.

When we pursue the unfamiliar, and begin anything new, we appear as awkward, unsure novices. These feelings of inadequacy and insecurity are primary reasons why so few people go "all in" to fulfill their highest aspirations. As you pursue your calling, always keep in mind that, there never was a winner, in any field, who was not once a beginner.

Opportunities Are Often in Plain Sight

At the Toastmasters Club, I met several staff members within our own in-company training organization. My company had an award-winning internal training institute, which offered comprehensive leadership and organizational development programs. I learned from the staff members that they were expanding their faculty.

As I grew more confident through my toastmasters' experience, and with my academic background in Management & Organizational Behavior, I was able to establish myself as a worthy candidate to become a faculty member.

Back to my MBA years, I decided not to chase what was popular, but to follow my interest in Management & Organizational Behavior. That decision proved to be very beneficial. You may discover, as I did, that every heartfelt choice you make will connect into a pattern and collectively move you toward your unique purpose. You may also discover that, with a clear vision, a strong faith, and a willingness to take actions, the door to your dreams will open up, in amazing yet unexpected ways.

My boss kindly supported me to pursue this passion in addition to my main job description activities. I attended the "Train the Trainer" program offered by DDI, an international firm specialized in human resources and leadership development, and became qualified as a Certified Facilitator. It was as if I had received a winning lottery ticket. I received my first training assignment right after the program. It was a three-day Management Essentials Program training in Hong Kong, with twenty middle level managers attending from five different Asian countries. I was to co-deliver four training modules with a local instructor.

When I received the huge pile of materials, including instructor manuals, student manuals and various worksheets, my flush of excitement turned into a panic attack. I only had a few weeks to prepare. How was I going to remember all the stuff? It was like preparing for a college entrance exam for the next few weeks. Because my regular job took almost all of my working day, I had to review the materials on evenings and weekends, and even on the flight to Hong Kong.

Arriving in the evening, I was welcomed by the enticing aroma of Hong Kong barbecue and the breathtaking skyline unique to Hong Kong Harbor. However, I was unable to sleep that night, partly because of jet leg and mostly because of nervous apprehension. I prayed that my brain wouldn't freeze as it did during my initial Toastmasters' event and I tried my best to visualize a confident image of myself.

As I walked into the classroom in the morning, the first thing I noticed was a magnificent mountain view through the huge glass windows. The lush forest in the background and my own positive expectations somehow alleviated my anxieties.

Amazingly, once I started to interact with the audience, I instantly enjoyed it and felt totally relaxed. The overall training turned out better than I had expected. We had a great time learning from and sharing with each other. The experience reinforced my interest and my confidence. I knew I was on the right path, because of how much I enjoyed this initial training involvement.

The pursuit of our calling is an ever-evolving process. As you move forward, you may encounter new alternatives and opportunities, sometimes coming disguised as challenges. What I have shared with you was just a beginning of my journey. Since then, I have had many opportunities to help people develop and grow. There were a lot of enjoyable, sparkling and heartwarming moments just as I had dreamed there would be. I relished the opportunities to inspire and be inspired, which happened on many occasions, such as the one that follows.

The Barrier of Loss Aversion

Realistically, most of us need to make a living and often have family responsibilities to deal with. As we pursue our dreams, we need to manage our reality wisely and responsibly. It is not a good idea to chase our dreams while leaving our children in survival mode.

Sometimes it's wise to take incremental steps toward our dreams. You may pursue them in spare time first, then part time and eventually full time, or you may take a step back before moving forward, starting part time while cutting back your spending to absolute necessities until you gradually build up a new income. I have taken incremental steps, over time, to pursue my own calling out of the same considerations. However, sooner or later, there will be a point where we need to leave behind what we had and make room for what we will have.

I once delivered a pricing training in Dongguan, China. During the program, I talked about how the psychology of "loss aversion" influenced pricing decisions and other decisions in life. The idea of "loss aversion" is that the pain of losing is much more powerful than the pleasure of gaining. At the group dinner, a participant came to me and shared how she thought about her own decisions in life in light of this concept. She had to give up what she had worked very hard for in order to pursue a new way of living.

As I listened to her story, I realized that, ultimately, pursuing our dreams is about giving up our old reality and replacing it with a new reality. As exciting as it sounds, the decision doesn't always come easily because the pain of giving up the old is too powerful compared to the pleasure of expecting a fresh, new direction that may result in major life fulfillment.

Every decision we make in life involves tradeoffs and risks. "Loss aversion" is also known as "risk aversion." That's why many people forever live in a structured life that feels safe and comfortable. The structure has a solid floor, which equates to a stable job, a nice house, and reliable income. However, this structured existence also has walls and, most importantly, a ceiling that limits the heights of our dreams and ambitions. By seeking security and avoiding risks, we may toil in jobs without passion, zest and joy. Dreams are suffocated because the thought of losing the solid floor and walls is too painful.

The lady at the training in Dongguan inspired me to consider how "loss aversion" influenced my own early decisions, and how I should continue to overcome this mental barrier to truly realize my potential. Meanwhile, I was very fortunate to meet an amazing couple who had overcome the barrier of "loss aversion" and transformed their lives in incredible ways.

Yuriy and Inna: Taking the Road Less Travelled

When focused on discovering my core passions, I began to learn about many seemingly ordinary individuals who had become extraordinary successes in a variety of endeavors. Each had decided to chase his or her passion, rather than a pension. Each came to a life-altering fork in the road, and instead of choosing the well-trodden path of least resistance, each took "the road less travelled." Inspired by Robert Frost's eloquent poem "The Road Not Taken," M. Scott Peck wrote one of the most iconic self-help books ever published, *The Road Less Travelled.*

One remarkable illustration of the meaning behind Robert Frost's quote, at the top of this chapter, involves Yuriy Yurchuk, the son-in-law of my daughters' piano teacher Galina. Yuriy was previously a finance professional specializing in mergers and acquisitions, and now is a rising baritone on the international opera stage.

When Galina shared with me the story of Yuriy and her daughter, Inna, I was so impressed that I asked for an opportunity to meet them. As an "Idealist," I always enjoy meeting and talking to people with amazing life

111

experiences. When they were back from London to Chicago for summer vacation, in spite of their busy schedules, we managed to meet late one night at a local Starbucks.

When we greeted each other, the first thing I noticed was Yuriy's deep, resonant speaking voice. As we talked about his transformation, I marveled at his remarkable journey. With a finance degree from a prestigious university in Ukraine, he was on an upward career path for nearly a decade as a merger and acquisition specialist with PriceWaterhouse Coopers (PwC). Then, incredibly, he transformed himself into a baritone, winning over audiences at the Royal Opera House in London.

Yuriy would have laughed at anyone who would have suggested that he embark on a professional singing path, after his transfer to the PwC Chicago office in 2010.

True enough, Yuriy's passion for music began in childhood. When he was fifteen years old, he wanted to study singing, but his teacher said he didn't have the innate talent and told him not to bother. Although the news was disappointing, his interest in music persisted. He loved to listen to music, to play the guitar and to sing. After settling in Chicago, he took singing lessons as a new hobby, with no intention of ever pursuing it as a career. His music teacher suggested that he should begin entering competitions so that he could receive feedback from the different panels of judges.

It was at one of these competitions that he met Professor Marc Embree from DePaul University. a former bass-baritone with the New York City Opera. This encounter was life-altering for Yuriy. Although Professor Embree had a long list of constructive criticisms concerning nearly every aspect of Yuriy's performance, he made one comment that was like a bolt out of the blue for the amateur singer. Professor Embree remarked that he had heard something that had caught his attention and encouraged him to begin classical music training.

Classical music training? Until age 28, Yuriy had never even been to an opera, let alone seriously consider himself leaning in that direction. In order to inspire him, Professor Embree took Yuriy to see a performance of Offenbach's *Les Contes d'Hoffmann* at the Lyric Opera of Chicago. Yuriy felt like he was watching a live performance of an epic motion picture. He was mesmerized by the artistic performances, the music and the overwhelming emotion filling the opera house. A few days later he met the lead singer from the opera at Professor Embree's place and, grudgingly, agreed to sing at that impromptu gathering of role models, who genuinely expressed their encouragement. And the rest, as they say, is history.

The Fork in the Road

Yuriy decisively changed his full-time job to part-time. He had five months to prepare before starting a formal Vocal Performance program at DePaul University School of Music. It was a special bachelor plus master's degree program designed for him, which condensed six years' study into three years. Without any formal training in music, he learned the basics in sight reading, piano, music theory and music history all within five months. Sometimes he studied fifteen hours a day.

Although it was extremely challenging, he felt comfortable in "wanting to" excel in learning the subjects instead of "having to" force himself to work through long hours of tedious details. He loved music, history and math. The musical theory was a lot like math to him. His passion, aptitude, and artistic personality were well aligned.

During his studies at DePaul University, he made his operatic debut as Marcello in *La Bohème*, followed by Ford in *Falstaff*. In 2014, He was one of five singers who were selected to join the Jette Parker Young Artists (JPYA) Program at the Royal Opera House in London, out of the

390 applicants from 58 countries. Meanwhile, he won multiple prizes in international singing competitions.

Although his journey was very different from my own, I could easily identify with him as a kindred spirit who also was breaking out of a structured chrysalis to fly as high and as far as he ever dared.

Yuriy talked about the importance for a singer to have a unique and recognizable voice. In singing, it's not just about how good you are, it's more about how unique you are. Of course, you need to meet world class standards and not become delusional about your talent. But once you find your voice, your mission should be to outperform yourself, rather than compete and compare yourself to others. Similarly, I believe that it's equally important for every one of us to have a unique, recognizable voice in life, and to develop that voice to the best of our abilities.

Compelled, Not Just Determined

I asked Yuriy, "When you made all the sacrifices, were you determined to make it work?" His answer really struck me. He said he was not "determined," but intrinsically "compelled" to keep doing it. More than fame, fortune or prestige, he believes that his internal, core passion has been much more motivating than any external pressures he may feel or rewards he may attain. Singing was an interest that just kept burning inside and growing in intensity with time, which is typical of a true passion or calling.

He experienced so many challenges that without this intrinsic, magnificent driving force that compelled him from within, he wouldn't have survived them. Professionally, one develops at a slow pace in music. It takes a long time to learn the repertoires and to build the skills, and the practices offstage are tedious and repetitive. After being accepted into JPYA program in 2014, Yuriy faced the challenge of keeping up with his colleagues, who had many years of professional training behind them. Because he started late, he had a much steeper climb.

Mentally, Yuriy also needed to overcome many challenges. There was stage fright. "I used to get nervous. During my first performances, I would go off the stage and not remember how it went," he recalls, "Not anymore, though!" There was rejection. A musician must have incredible resilience as the rejections are crazy. Fifteen auditions may at best result in one successful role. There was the unusual subjectivity about the concept of talents. One may tell you that your voice was not powerful enough, until another decision-maker was enamored with your voice. The critics were impressed and suddenly the less powerful voice was no longer a problem.

These all sounded difficult and challenging, but surprisingly, Yuriy has walked his journey with incredible joy. Many of us grow up with the belief that achieving success requires relentless pain, suffering, tunnel vision and selfish ambition. As a result, we may struggle for years and even reach some of our goals, but end up exhausted, unfulfilled and with our lives out of balance.

As Deepak Chopra observes in his transformational work, *The Seven Spiritual Laws of Success,* "Such desperate striving isn't necessary or even desirable. In the natural world, creation comes forth with ease. A seed doesn't struggle to become a tree—it simply unfolds in grace. You can fulfill your deepest desires with effortless joy." There is no doubt that achieving success requires a lot of hard work, but when you work to become who you are designed to be, you work with joy and passion rather than pains and struggles.

"Is This It for Me?"

As Yuriy's life took a dramatic turn, their move to London created a perfect opportunity for his wife, Inna, to pursue her calling as well. Inna was artistic and creative as a child. Her mom, our piano teacher Galina, took her to galleries, concerts, and musical programs to nurture and expand her interests in the arts. However, she pursued math as college major in order to have a stable job and a secure future. Just as her husband to be had, she became a financial professional upon graduation.

Although on a successful career path, she asked herself, "Is this it for me?" This uneasiness continued to grow in intensity. To relieve the anxiety, she started to study dancing, art and then photography. Just as a passion for singing grew stronger and stronger for Yuriy, a passion for photography grew stronger and stronger for Inna. After they moved to London, she became a professional photographer. When I saw her photographs, I instantly fell in love with them. As she beautifully described, her pictures were like her favorite type of food, fresh, organic, and natural.

In many ways, Yuriy and Inna gave up a lot in order to move on. They left the stable and high-income positions behind without fully knowing what the future would hold. It's not easy to go for an artistic career, as romantic as it appears, forfeiting a stable income to bet on a dream. Nevertheless, they left a comfortable, structured environment and overcame the barrier of "loss aversion," because their dreams were big and their passions were strong. Most importantly, as Yuriy put it, "If you enjoy work, you won't work for one day anymore. It's safe in risking doing something you enjoy!"

As we explore the biographies of people who have changed the world for the better, some of them became rich and famous. However, the majority of them did not. Many of the most prolific, positive role models throughout history simply found their callings and were so dedicated and motivated by their core passions that they would have committed themselves to their causes for only the basic necessities. Their intrinsic pursuit of excellence was stronger than their desire for status and money, as is the case for Yuriy and Inna, and the case for Vanessa and Tao.

As I maneuver the day to day responsibilities as a wife and mother, filled with music lessons, recitals, homework, horseback riding, sporting events, church, school activities... I try to take time to observe how my daughters, Audrey and Brooke, respond to different activities and events in life. What lights up their spirits with the most joy and anticipation? What are their greatest challenges and frustrations?

I suppose I could have written this chapter with this simple wish: as we discover our own way to view our life's work as play, let us also be a source of inspiration and help guide our children to view their life's work as play. Let us chase our passion, not just our pension. And take the road less travelled.

9

Children Have Their Own Destinies

Your children are not your children. They are the sons and daughters of Life's longing for itself. They come through you but not from you. And though they are with you, yet they belong not to you.
—*Kahlil Gibran*

For parents reading this book, in addition to discovering who we are, we may want to help our children discover, develop and express who they are.

For my own daughters, I have been observing their temperament through our daily interactions. I have also been introducing them to as many extracurricular activities as they are willing to experience. I am able to observe in what areas they show natural talents and interests in this process. The introduction doesn't have to be in the form of enrolling them in classes. Taking them to a concert, a gallery or a sporting event can all be helpful.

Personally, I wouldn't recommend that my daughters take professional temperament or aptitude assessments until they are old enough to consider college majors and career interests. As much as I want to help them discover and develop their natural talents, I don't want them to prematurely label themselves. I hope that they have a balanced childhood and explore as many different activities as they are interested in exploring.

Children May Have Different Talents

Children don't always inherit natural talents from their father or mother. Parents who are accomplished and talented in a profession may be frustrated to discover that their children are unable to carry their torch forward, such as the mom in the mother-daughter story earlier and the dad in the father-son story below.

One young man was unable to follow his famous surgeon father's footsteps because he hesitated too much during simple surgical procedures. What his father falsely branded as cowardice actually was the lack of tweezer dexterity. Although the son tried very hard to learn the skills, he had not inherited his father's tweezer dexterity and other traits fundamental to becoming a precise, steady-handed surgeon.

Before parents set their hearts on children following their footsteps, they should check whether their children have the aptitudes to succeed in that career, well before the children enter serious majors in college. The surgeon father could have checked his son's aptitudes in tweezer dexterity, hand-eye coordination and structural visualization before sending him toward a surgeon career.

It's worth mentioning that the aptitudes required for many careers may change in the future. Robots have already been engaged in performing surgeries in some areas. Maybe someday the tweezer dexterity aptitude will no longer be a concern for certain requirements of the surgical profession. As parents, we want to be up-to-date about the aptitudes required for our children's potential career choices.

It can be frustrating for some parents who have been successful in achieving their dreams to see their children pursue a drastically different path. A real estate executive paved a perfect path for his daughter. If she had followed his calling and example, she would have had the best starting position, ready-made network, and resources that other young people could only dream of. However, his daughter decided to be an animal trainer, because of her passion and gift in working with animals.

It can be even more frustrating for parents when their children demonstrate "special" gifts and interests that go beyond the parents' comfort zone. Jason Wu has been recognized as one of the brightest stars in the fashion world. He liked Barbie dolls when he was a little boy. He would ask his parents to buy Barbies for him. He would then take them apart, remake their clothes and restyle their hair and looks. In an interview, he said that he had over 150 dolls in his collection.

As an Asian parent, I knew how unnerved most Asian parents would feel if their boy showed this kind of interest. Fortunately, he had brave and supportive parents. Both his mom and his dad bought him dolls.

He said about his dad, "It was so against everything he believes and understands, but he did it anyway." Jason Wu's success can't be separated from his parents' unconditional love and understanding. I can't help wondering, if he had been born into a family where his parents suppressed his gift and interest, how different his destiny might have been.

When there is a seed in our children, it will seek to grow and blossom. The best thing we can do as parents is to support and facilitate the expression of the seed. Children and parents are unique individuals. We want to respect our children's uniqueness as much as we respect our own, allowing them to listen to and follow their own drumbeats, no matter how far afield from our aspirations.

Respect but Guide Their Interests

We may or may not be able to confirm what our children's dominant passion is, but we usually can observe the activities in which they are interested. When it comes to children's interests, we as parents want to introduce our children to the rich banquet that lies ahead for them, and then allow the children to order from the menu based on their own tastes. However, while we respect their interests, we also want to guide their interests because of the unique challenges children face.

Children are usually eager to identify themselves with a particular peer group, rather than make their own personal judgments. They face many temptations today and can easily be influenced to develop interests that may or may not be healthy for them.

Taking video games as an example, some children may have a genuine talent in creating games; some children may benefit from educational games as a way to facilitate learning; and some children may simply be wasting time in addictive playing. If a child happens to be obsessed, be open enough, yet vigilant and wise enough, to determine whether there is a true programming talent, an educational opportunity or simply an addiction driven behavior.

The other challenge is that children are not mature enough to have the level of discipline and patience that they may have in adult life. It takes time and effort to develop a talent, but children don't always enjoy the work even if they are interested in an activity. Even Martha Argerich, a legendary pianist, admitted that she loved to play piano but disliked practice as a child. She pretended to be practicing, but instead sat at the piano reading books like *Uncle Tom's Cabin* hidden on her lap.

My daughter, Audrey, has taken piano lessons since she was six. She is interested in piano and demonstrates a fair amount of natural talent. However, there were several times when she claimed that she was no longer interested in piano and she wanted to quit. I struggled to understand whether she genuinely lost interest in playing piano or she lost interest due to other factors, such as reluctance to practice or pressure from our expectations.

When I put her lessons on hold, from time to time, she still sat before the piano and played with great passion. It became clear to me that deep inside, she was still interested in playing. We worked out a new plan each time so that she could proceed in a way in which she was most comfortable.

Today she has a solid foundation in piano which she will be able to carry and enjoy throughout her life. In spite of the episodes of struggles, she thanks me for recognizing her talent and interest, guiding her to grow but not letting her quit or pushing her to compete. As she grows, she increasingly appreciates the beauty of music. She continues to express herself more and more through music, even improvising and creating her own pieces.

Interest based on natural talent is a gift given to a child. Just as every diamond needs to be polished, a child needs to be encouraged and trained in order to be able to express that gift. An art teacher told me about a teenage boy who was constantly frustrated when he first came to her studio. The boy had great imagination and creativity, but he was unable to express those inner impressions due to a lack of techniques. She mentioned that many artists, like Pablo Picasso, actually had solid techniques in spite of their abstract art styles.

Several years ago, the book *Battle Hymn of the Tiger Mother*, authored by Amy Chua, stirred up heated discussions about parenting. Because of my Chinese heritage, I have encountered many "tiger moms" from my childhood through my motherhood. These "tiger moms" are strict and demanding, pushing their children to the highest possible standard in all the activities they pursue.

Although I don't see myself as a "tiger mom," I echo the belief that parents need to be proactive instead of overly permissive. As we help our children develop their talents and interests, we want to instill proper work ethics and shape them into responsible individuals who can function effectively in the future and realize their potential. One of our missions as parents is to nurture the quality of empowerment, rather than one of entitlement.

Seek Fulfillment Through Ourselves, Not Our Children

When we guide our children, the guidance should be based on the children's talents, interests, inner desires and aspirations, rather than for the external sake of proving their worth and even our own worth by watching them win medals.

Our children should not be viewed as vehicles to achieve our own unfulfilled dreams and meet our own unfilled needs. There are those fathers who fantasize that their sons will grow up to be the sports' stars that the fathers could never become. And there are the well-meaning mothers who long for their daughters to wear the crowns of beauty queens that the mothers wished for, but never realized.

There are parents, especially moms, who give up their own goals and invest all of their time and energy in their children. Some moms make the choice out of love because their children have special needs. Some moms enjoy this lifestyle, which, to their credit, can be very fulfilling. However, some moms give this attention grudgingly and expect their children to make up for their own unfulfilled goals. They are not hesitant to remind their children of this sacrifice whenever the children miss expectations.

If I were a child, I wouldn't want to live with such guilt and pressure. I would rather have my parents pursue their goals, act as my role models and give me space to grow.

As parents, we want to seek fulfillment through our own actions and contributions, rather than try to accomplish our own dreams or relive our past triumphs, vicariously, through our children. *"On Children,"* one of my favorite poems from Kahlil Gibran's beautiful book of poetry, *The Prophet,* perfectly describes our roles with our children. I hope you will be inspired by this poem as I have been.

Establish Healthy Self-esteem in Our Children

Every child is born with more potential than he or she will ever need, however, without proper care and guidance, the early years can easily diminish children's self-esteem. Younger children's self-esteem largely comes from the acceptance and care of their parents. Most psychologists say it starts in infancy. If parents do not accept the baby as he or she really is, and are not responsive to the baby's needs, tiny infants can feel that their demands are excessive, burdensome, not worthy of full attention. They learn to withdraw and over time respond by asking for less and, worse, expecting less.

Comparison then enters the equation as soon as they're old enough to compare themselves with others or be compared to others. Once it starts, the erosion of self-esteem often picks up speed in high school, when there is a greater amount of peer comparison and peer pressure. As stated by Dr. James C. Dobson, founder of Focus on the Family, "Comparison is the root of all feelings of inferiority. The moment you begin examining other people's strengths against your most obvious weaknesses, your self-esteem starts to crumble."

Comparison also happens among parents. Many parents, especially in our Asian culture, feel anxiety, panic and even shame when their children fall short academically, even if the children have put in a lot of hard work. Many parents also feel the same way when their children display a personality that is not popular, such as being shy and introverted. This kind of tension often causes painful conflicts between frustrated parents and dutiful, but uniquely different children.

To help our children establish healthy self-esteem and stand strong in the face of peer comparison, we want to instill the inner value from their early years that each of them is a unique and precious creation. Their mission is not to become others, but to become the best version of themselves.

As I have taught my children, all children have their own natural strengths and limitations, which may be revealed at different points in life. They should never consider anyone, including themselves, inferior or superior based on a single dimension, whether it's in academics, extracurricular activities, or other areas of life. We are grateful for the gifts given to us. We are also appreciative of the gifts that other children have received. It's the difference in each of us that makes the world fun and interesting.

As parents, we want to have a positive vision and an unshakable faith in our children. Every child has unique gifts which can lead them to succeed in unique ways. In the infinitely abundant world, there are ample places and opportunities that can make the best use of our children's gifts. Every child also has her or his own timing to blossom. There are more than enough examples of people who are not being noticed as children but become hugely successful as adults.

While we all are seeking growth and improvement in our children, it's better to focus on discovering and developing their gifts rather than fixing their limitations. We help our children achieve their potential by accepting, appreciating, loving them as unique individuals, and by allowing them to express who they are created to be.

10

What Is Your Health Philosophy?

> You are as important to your health
> as your health is to you.
> —*Terri Guillemets*

Nothing is more vital than living a healthy life, because it affects everything else we do in life, including the ability to live our unique calling and to reach our full potential. Health is an important foundation for freedom. As Swiss philosopher Henri Frederic Amiel said, "In health there is freedom. Health is the first of all liberties."

I became passionate about health after I suffered from a sub-health condition and realized that the traditional medical approach wouldn't help me much. Over the years, I have studied extensively about every aspect of healthy living. My health has been transformed after I followed a personalized health approach, rooted in my health philosophy.

I don't presume to be an expert on health and only offer you my humble thoughts as they apply to my own health. To me, health is an extremely personal matter and should be treated as such. I don't believe there is one philosophy and one approach working for all.

My intention in sharing my journey is to open your perspectives on your own unique situation and to make you aware of the power you have concerning your health, no matter what your situation is today. I am an explorer, not a scientist or a medical professional. It is my hope that you will fully investigate what applies to you and what you believe works best for you.

Health Definition Leads to Health Destination

Consciously or unconsciously, people hold different definitions of health. Some consider health as being free of diseases. Some consider health as a purely physical matter. I see health as "a state of complete physical, mental and social well-being and not merely the absence of disease or infirmity," as defined by the World Health Organization.

To me, the primary goal of healthy living is to maintain the body's balance and harmony, and to restore it when the balance or harmony is broken. When there are health problems, I will consult a qualified physician to address them. Meanwhile, I am more concerned about finding and treating the root causes, whether they apply to diet, nutrition, exercise, mental or environmental factors, instead of simply suppressing the symptoms.

Many people today are satisfied with suppressing the symptoms with medicine, without a holistic plan for a fundamental health transformation. This common approach is called, in Chinese terms, "Treating the head when the head aches; treating the foot when the foot aches." This approach not only makes it difficult to restore the body's natural harmony and achieve true, sustainable health, it could also lead to many harmful side effects in the long run.

Some people take prescription drugs for the rest of their lives, especially for the chronic degenerative diseases such as high blood pressure, atherosclerosis, and diabetes. Yet it may be possible to improve or even reverse these conditions if people are committed to address the root causes in their lifestyles. For example, type 2 diabetes is often, if not always, related to overweight and insulin resistance, which could potentially be addressed through diet, nutrition, exercise and other lifestyle changes. Although physicians can treat diseases, we ourselves, through our choices, have more power to make ourselves healthy than we have believed possible.

Although life span is one of the indicators of health, to me, a healthy life is about quality as much as quantity. Many people today die after long battles with chronic degenerative diseases. Even when there is virtually no vitality left, people can extend their lives for many years with the advancement in medicine and medical technologies. As normal as the phenomenon has become, that's not the way it is supposed to be.

When I was a child, I often heard stories like this: a monk passed away at age 95 when he was meditating; or an elder passed away at 90 while he was taking a nap. They lived a healthy and balanced life until the moment they came to the natural ending of their lives. I consider such a peaceful death, at an old age, free of pain and suffering, the most blessed form of completing our mortal journey.

Although we now live in a different age and environment, I still believe that it's possible to live healthy and die at an old age, being free of degenerative disease, if we hold the right health philosophy and follow the right health approach.

Your Mind Influences Your Body

When we talk about health, we mostly think in terms of physical health. However, mental health is a critical part of our overall well-being. It also has a direct impact on our physical health. According to some research, its impact to physical health might be even more significant than the impact of lifestyles.

Although we have much to learn about the brain and the central nervous system, we already know of the binding relationship between mind and body. Thoughts and images have an unmistakable, measurable physical reaction. To put it another way, what the mind focuses on, the body expresses.

When our fear and worry turn into anxiety, we suffer distress. Distress activates our endocrine system, changing the production of hormones and antibodies. Our immune system becomes less effective; our resistance levels are lowered; we become more vulnerable to bacteria, viruses, and other ever-present hazards.

Studies have found strong correlations between emotions, personalities and diseases. Howard S. Friedman, Professor of Psychology at the University of California, Riverside, has researched the relationship between personality and health, and identified the "disease-prone personalities" and "self-healing personalities."

The disease-prone personalities are associated with pervasive negative moods, such as depression, anxiety, and irritability. People with disease-prone personalities tend to dwell on the negatives in life and are often dissatisfied. Self-healing personalities are associated with being conscientious, emotionally secure, having enthusiasm for life, and strong social relationships. People with self-healing personalities tend to dwell on the positives of life and are often content.

Within the disease-prone personalities, certain personalities are more prone to certain diseases, which have spawned terms such as heart disease prone personalities, cancer prone personalities. Some of the heart disease prone personalities are aggressiveness, over-competitiveness, impatience, and hostility. Some of the cancer prone personalities are resentment, pessimism, guilt, and being "too nice."

Being "too nice" is the tendency to suppress emotions, be overly self-sacrificing, and constantly try to please other people. "Too nice" and "true nice" sound similar but they are fundamentally different. "True nice" actions are expressed out of love, which is the root of positive emotions; while "too nice" actions are expressed out of fear and insecurity, which is the root of negative emotions.

I was born with a mellow disposition. As I grew up, my parents taught me to always focus on the big picture instead of petty stuff, positives instead of negatives, solutions instead of complaints. Because of their influence, I have generally held a positive mindset toward life. It has served me well in my career, my relationships as well as in my health. However, an unexpected challenge occurred about fifteen years ago. The experience taught me the importance of having purpose and meaning in life.

It was a typical hot and humid day in Houston. In spite of the blazing sunshine, I was feeling down and dark inside. It had been going on for months. I suffered from insomnia night after night. Nothing seemed interesting to me. Nothing gave me pleasure, even my favorite food and TV shows.

I felt anxiety over little things. I was nervous about the bad news on TV. I worried about the little issues my clients raised. I felt overwhelmed for a whole week when I had a minor car accident, which only broke a side mirror. Physically, I felt that the energy was sucked out of me. I didn't want to do anything beyond what I had to do.

On this day, it occurred to me that maybe something was wrong with me. I had felt down in the past but never this persistent and this dark. I jumped online and typed my symptoms one by one: loss of interest, feeling down and hopeless, anxiety over little things, insomnia, low energy... I was shocked and scared to discover that I had slipped into a state of depression.

My life seemed perfect on the outside. I had a decent career, a beautiful house, and a caring husband. Because I didn't have children yet, I had a lot of free time that I can only dream of having today. However, on the inside, I felt I had reached a permanent plateau in my life. I didn't see meaning in life other than going through the motions. The sense of emptiness gradually took root in my mind.

It was the darkest time in my life. Every morning, as I drove toward the east to work, I could feel my heart sink as the sun rose. In spite of these awful feelings, being an "Idealist," I was determined to break out of this vicious mental prison.

I painstakingly studied everything I could find about depression. The philosophy of Morita therapy helped me greatly in the process. This philosophy involves decentralizing self, grounding actions in purpose of each moment, and living harmoniously with the feelings instead of attempting to fight them off. It enabled me to live with peace in the midst of hardship. I joked with my depression every morning, as if I were talking to a friend, "My friend, we are in each other's company again, but someday you will be bored and leave me behind."

As it is said, behind every curse is a blessing. I shared my depression with only one person, my friend Lilian. I knew she could understand what I was going through. Lilian was about the same age as my parents. She came from Suriname, a country in South America. She was a woman of strong faith, with a warm, joyful personality and a big, loving heart. In addition to serving at local ministries, she traveled globally to serve at ministries across South America, Europe and Asia. She changed many lives, including my own, with her faith, wisdom and incredible capacity to love.

For nearly two years when we were together, Lilian was like a mother to me. She loved me, encouraged me and prayed for me every day. In spite of my depressed mood, surprisingly, some of my best memories were from that time period.

Lilian and her husband, Frits, were both great at cooking. A reflection of their diverse cultural background, their cooking had a fusion flair and integrated the flavor of Surinam, Tex-Mex, Indonesia and Vietnam. We had wonderful times cooking and sharing together. Their friendship was tremendously uplifting for me. My interest in cooking was also inspired during that time. I found that cooking, as a creative activity, had a soothing and therapeutic effect.

When my husband was traveling, Lilian was afraid that I would feel lonely and depressed. She often came over to cook with me and give me moral support. We had long, deep conversations about life. Her rich life experiences and her God-given wisdom made a profound impact on my world view and my value system.

I realized that up to that point, I had lived a small, self-centered life with a narrow vision. I didn't have a compelling purpose in life other than making myself live comfortably and look good in others' eyes. In spite of my positive self-image to the world outside, I felt hollow and stifled on the inside.

Although I didn't believe in God at the time, I experienced God's grace through Lilian. Her love and prayers eventually led me to my faith. It was the beginning of a lifelong transformation. As I began a personal relationship with God, my vision was enlarged and I discovered a higher purpose in life.

I was inspired to live a big life as Lilian was living—a life in which I would always look up—seeking divine guidance; look forward—living with passion and hope; and, most importantly, look outside—helping others and contributing to society. I was very blessed to have Lilian as my role model. When I had my moments of doubts and lows in life, I often asked myself, "What would Lilian say to me in this situation?"

As I found a new meaning for my life, I felt a renewed sense of joy, passion and enthusiasm. My friend named "depression" lost its power over me and gradually left me behind. My sense of purpose has become more and more concrete over time, especially as I have progressed through my journey of self-discovery.

I want to become the best version of myself as God has designed me to be. I want to help others and contribute to society using my unique gifts. I want to be a role model for my children. I want to take the best care of all my loved ones. There are so many wonderful things to look forward to that I literally have no bandwidth to worry about the petty things anymore.

Each of us has a different purpose or mission in life, which may change as we move through different stages of life. It may be to raise healthy and independent children. It may be to take care of our aging parents. It may be to change lives through charity work. No matter what our purpose is, big or small, it fuels us to live and to survive.

Purpose is the engine that powers our lives. I was once told a remarkable story about a grandpa who was gravely ill but miraculously recovered after his son and daughter-in-law died in a tragic accident. He survived because he had a powerful, new purpose in life, which was to raise his grandchildren.

When I was a teenager, I thought it was a dream life to play and watch TV every day without having to study or work. Today I continue to value freedom, but I no longer consider it a blessing to watch TV or party every day. I want to live with passion and purpose throughout my life.

As a personal observation, also based upon my own experience with depression, many people develop physical and emotional problems not because they are too busy or too challenged, but because they are too empty and have lost purpose in life.

There are people, from young adults to seniors, who have few responsibilities in life, an abundance of money and free time, but no exciting purpose or vision going forward. They are easily swallowed by emptiness or petty inconveniences and become prone to physical, emotional and mental problems.

There are others who have many more responsibilities and remain active throughout their lives. They may be business leaders, public figures, mothers in a big family, or in many other different roles. Because they live with purpose and passion, they often end up living long and happy.

Our minds are like gardens. If we don't feed them with fresh plantings of purpose, the soil will become barren. If we don't cultivate and nourish them daily with positive thoughts and actions, the weeds of pettiness will grow and flourish. I wish that we all could live like sunflowers, rooted in purpose and passion, and always smiling toward the sun.

Wisdom from My Father:
Overcome Nature with Nurture

Genetics play an important role in our health. We are born with DNA inherited from our parents and ancestors, including our predispositions to certain health conditions, aging factors and diseases. When you make an appointment with a new physician or visit a new medical clinic, you are given a set of questions on a clipboard. There are usually two sets of questions: one set asks about the health history of your close relatives, and the other queries you about your own health history.

Even with all the technological advances today, understanding what your other family members have experienced throughout their lives and comparing those experiences with your own is still a valid method of physiological self-discovery.

I have spent time to learn the medical history of both my mom's and my dad's families, so that I am aware of the risks that I may face at some point in my life.

In addition to family history, genetic testing services can help people learn more about their genetic heritage and risks. There are different types of genetic testing serving different purposes. The predictive testing can provide information about a person's risk of developing a specific disorder or disease. However, the intricacies lie in the interpretation of the results, and usually there is not a clear path as far as exactly what you should do with the result.

I most likely wouldn't venture into this type of testing unless I have confidence that the results can be properly interpreted, and most importantly, I know exactly how to act on the result.

Personally, I have found it challenging to deal with the "probability" of health risks. During my pregnancy, I had to decide whether I should do an amniotic fluid test after a positive screening test result. I was torn between the two set of probabilities: the probability of the baby carrying a problem, and the probability of the risks from an amniotic fluid test. I eventually took the test and luckily everything turned out fine, but the anxiety over the probabilities was one of the worst anxieties I had experienced.

Even knowing the probability of a genetic risk, most people, like me, probably aren't courageous enough to take radical preventative actions as the actress Angelina Jolie did. Angelina Jolie had a preventative double mastectomy and preventive removal of her ovaries and fallopian tubes after she discovered a mutation of the BRCA1 gene, which significantly raises her risks of both breast and ovarian cancer.

I am more comfortable with prevention through my daily lifestyle and, therefore, prefer to live a healthier lifestyle in the here and now, without carrying the anxieties about the probabilities of experiencing future disease.

The extent of the influence from genes varies depending on the specific type of diseases. But the good news is, according to studies, genetics in general only account for approximately 20% to 30% of an individual's chance of surviving to age 85. Healthy lifestyles can greatly mitigate the genetic risks. Again, no matter what you discover in "your nature," you can always have a positive impact in all aspects of your life through "your nurture."

My dad is a great example of this. He was not only born with a poor genetic inheritance, but also lived through many traumatic events in his younger years. He was born during the Chinese Civil War. His mom grew up in a well-to-do family, but unfortunately the family fortunes did not continue as she matured. She married into a poor farming family. Because she was unskilled in both housework and farm work, she was treated badly by her husband and mother-in-law. After bearing five children, she became very ill with an undiagnosed disease.

My dad was the youngest of the five children. When he was a baby, his mom literally threw him away several times, partly because of her depressed mental state, and partly because of the severe food shortage. His older sister searched for him and brought him back home each time.

During one, final time, she found him wrapped in a blanket, nearly frozen on the bank of an icy creek, on a cold winter day. She decided to hide him in a barn, with a horse as his only companion. His sister raised him with sorghum flour mixed with water, until his mom became too ill to force him out of their home.

He was four years old when his mother passed away. When he was ten years old, his dad died from esophageal cancer. When he was thirty years old, his most beloved sister, who saved his life, died as a result of heart disease. When he was fifty years old, his dearest brother passed away from lung cancer.

In spite of his poor genetic inheritance, a malnourished childhood, and a continuing series of emotional traumas, my dad grew up to be a healthy, kind and productive man. As I write this book, he is seventy years of age, yet looks much younger than his peers. When we reflected on his life experiences, we agreed that three factors contributed most to his well-being.

He is very much in tune with his body. Unlike many men who pay little attention to their health, he knows the importance of health because of the painful experiences of his early family life. He is keenly aware of his genetic vulnerabilities. As much as possible, he proactively takes care of his health weak spots through natural and holistic methods.

When I was a child, he often offered steamed Chinese yams on our dinner plates, which are considered to be natural foods that enhance digestive functions. When he experienced insomnia, instead of taking sleeping pills, he learned various relaxation techniques and massages to provide relief. In addition, he diligently follows a positive lifestyle, such as balanced diet, moderate exercise, and avoiding harmful substances like alcohol and cigarettes.

The other factor is that he has a very positive attitude toward life. In spite of the many adversities in his life, he has remained grateful for all that he has been granted. He has never held a grudge against his mother, preferring to understand her pain and suffering. He is always grateful to her for giving him life. He never complains about how unfair life has been in the past, but remains optimistic about the future.

Although my dad didn't know the idea of prayer until recent years, I believe he has essentially blessed both my brother and me with his positive and uplifting thoughts about us. He has a loving heart and genuinely cares for everyone around him; this has been constant throughout his teaching career and beyond. To this day he is respected and loved by students, family and friends regardless of the passing of time.

Last but not least, he enjoys life and loves to learn new things. When he was a college student, he was part of the school's singing and dancing ensemble. When I was a child, he planted and took care of a variety of flowers and fruit trees in our little courtyard. I especially loved the grape trees and the pomegranate trees in the harvest season.

After he retired, he often came to visit my family in the U.S. He studied English every day with the elementary level English textbooks and recordings. After I came back home from work, he was always prepared with his list of questions.

My dad is my inspiration as I continue to refine my own health philosophy and approach. His experience tells me that a healthy lifestyle and an attitude of optimism can play a crucial role in one's health. To a great extent, they can mitigate the genetic risks as well as the health damages done in the past.

As we become more aware of our physical characteristics, including genetic risks, we can make conscious, strategic lifestyle choices to nurture ourselves and protect us from the risks. It's never too late to design a healthy lifestyle for yourself.

Healthy Lifestyles Can Be Enjoyable

We want to live healthy in an enjoyable and sustainable way by incorporating our unique personalities and preferences into our lifestyles. Some people may prefer a precise and scientific health regimen. To these individuals, it is important to count the calorie intake, to track the servings of fruits and vegetables, and to follow a well-planned exercise program in a gym. Others, like me, may prefer a much more relaxed approach.

Some of you may laugh at that statement. As you read this book, including this chapter, it may seem to you that there is nothing relaxed about my approach to life, because

I have engaged in so many readings, research investigations, and reflections.

As said in Chinese philosophy, learning is a process where you must go from simplicity to complexity and then from complexity back to simplicity. The first simplicity is the result of innocence or ignorance, but the second simplicity is the result of enlightenment and clarity. As I share with you the groundwork that I have done, in great details, it's not meant to overwhelm you, but meant to lead you to the second point of simplicity.

Returning to my approach to lifestyles, I prefer a less structured health regimen that follows the three themes: common sense, simplicity and pleasure.

Common sense is as simple as mirroring the way our grandparents lived when they were children, before food and fitness were industrialized. They ate fruits and vegetables that were organic, fresh, seasonal, and naturally ripened. Their meat, fish, chicken came from fresh catch. Their grocery bags were filled with real food, not cans.

They exercised through their daily chores. They didn't drive around the mall to find the closest parking space, or take an elevator in a two-story building, and then save all the walks for the gym. Health and fitness were naturally and seamlessly integrated into every aspect of their lives.

Simplicity means to follow the right principles but not get wrapped up in the mind-boggling details such as calories, heart rates, steps, inches, pounds. One could live by the "zipper test" instead of measuring waist circumference every day. Simplicity also means minimum time, effort and complexity. This is important for moms like me, as our time is already stretched thin between family, work and other competing priorities.

Pleasure means to seek enjoyment from what we eat and what we do. It's not sustainable if we live a lifestyle that feels like labor instead of pleasure. Occasional indulgence is fine. It's all about balance and quality. I enjoy nice dinners, but I balance those special occasions with a fruit-based lunch the next day. I enjoy fried food, but I only have them in restaurants. I enjoy a few pieces of fine candies, but only at special times. When we combine balance and quality, we will have much more freedom to derive pleasure in life while still staying healthy.

Your Health Needs to Be "Your Way"

Because each of us has different physical characteristics, we need a personalized approach as we develop healthy lifestyles.

Growing up in China, I was aware of the rich heritage of health philosophies rooted in thousands of years of Chinese medicine traditions. A theme of these philosophies is the recognition that people are born with different physical characteristics. What the Chinese discovered thousands of years ago is that one size, one amount, one nutrition plan, or one exercise regimen does not fit all. Even the widely accepted good health practices may not suit everyone.

A friend of mine was born with what's called, in Chinese medicine terms, a "cold and wet" physical condition. Bombarded by popular health advice, she started to drink eight glasses of water a day, plus adding a lot more fruits and raw vegetables in her diet. Instead of feeling healthier, she felt worse because the new habit made her already "cold and wet" condition even "colder and wetter." She eventually realized that her body couldn't handle this and had to devote a major effort to repair the damage.

Although western cultures believed for many centuries that general health prescriptions and lifestyle choices were adequate for most populations, scientific research today, throughout the world, has also confirmed that there needs to be a personalized approach to health and longevity. Personalization, or customization, is the theme of the future. It is also at the forefront of wellness and disease prevention practices.

At the most basic level, men and women have different nutrition needs. Women need to watch their calcium and iron levels more closely than men do. Children, adults and seniors have different needs for exercise. Intense exercises that are good for a young or middle-aged adult can be detrimental to a senior.

People living in different parts of the world have different diet needs. The traditional Caribbean diet fulfills many of the balanced nutrition guidelines recommended by the U.S. Department of Agriculture. It's rich in seafood, a variety of fruits and vegetables and lean protein, while being low in refined grains, sugar and salt. However, this type of diet is not practical for people living in the northern-most arctic regions of the world.

In addition to these basic differences, each individual is different in his or her specific physical characteristics. Just as our personalities are shaped by both inborn temperament and the environment, our physical characteristics are shaped by both inborn biological traits, or genetic makeup, and the lifestyles we have experienced. We are on a much better path to achieve true health if we have more insights into our unique physical characteristics, and then nurture our body with a personalized health approach.

11

Ideal Diet: The Diet That Is Right for You

> You should have personalized genomics, personalized physiology, personalized medicine, where each person's different, and each body is an integrated whole.
> —*George M. Church*

An important part of my health philosophy is that there has to be a personalized approach as we develop healthy lifestyles, because each of us has different physical characteristics. An integral part of "know thyself" is to discover these physical characteristics and develop personalized healthy lifestyles accordingly. When it comes to diet, we are what we eat, and we also want to eat as we are.

I once participated in a health and education retreat in a beautiful facility on the oceanfront in Baja California, Mexico, specializing in functional medicine. Functional Medicine addresses the underlying causes of disease with a holistic and systematic approach. It addresses the whole person, not just an isolated set of symptoms.

During the retreat, I experienced the most comprehensive healthy lifestyles first hand, including diet, nutrition, detoxification, fitness, massage therapy, psycho-spiritual programs and healthy environments. I benefited greatly from its nutritional advisor program. As part of the program, I learned three important principles about diet and have since applied in my own life.

Develop Your Personalized Diet Plan

The first diet principle is to understand the various diets, such as the blood type diet, metabolic type diet and other diet plans, and incorporate some of the best principles from each to form your ideal diet.

You can find many kinds of diet plans on the market today. Some of them are based on physical type analysis. A physical type analysis defines different physical types based on a set of physical characteristics. Each physical type usually has its own health advantages and risks, and the ideal diet, exercise, and other lifestyles considerations associated with it.

Depending on the culture, the region and the medical tradition, there are many different ways to look at physical types. Some physical type analyses are more sophisticated and typically require professional evaluation. The traditional Chinese medicine identifies people into nine common physical types, including the "cold and wet" type as I mentioned earlier. The system has been established and validated through thousands of years of experience.

The other physical type analyses, such as blood type analysis and metabolic type analysis, are more straight forward and easier to understand. These physical type analyses have their limitations and often involve some level of controversies. They may apply very well in some people but not as well in others. The conclusions between different kinds of analyses sometimes conflict with each other.

Although this is often a source of confusion, it is understandable because our bodies are highly complex, individualized, and influenced by numerous genetic and lifestyle factors. It's impossible for any generalized theory to address the vast amount of individual differences.

Personally, I consider these physical type analyses as thought-provoking tools which I can use to expand my health vocabulary, guide my self-reflection and bring myself to a higher plateau of self-awareness. It's similar to my approach in discovering my natural temperament and strengths.

Physical type analyses can be useful tools to offer insight into our physical characteristics and to help us refine our lifestyles. But you should always take the results with a grain of salt, and ultimately, listen to your body to determine what works or does not work for you.

On the blood type analysis, I was enlightened by the book, *Eat Right 4 Your Type: The Individualized Blood Type Diet® Solution,* authored by Dr. Peter J. D'Adamor. According to this book, different blood types reflect different internal chemistries, and, consequently, call for different approaches to healthy lifestyles, such as diet, exercise, stress management, disease prevention and treatment. This book gives a list of highly beneficial foods, neutral foods, and foods to avoid for each blood type.

As I compared the list for different blood types, I began to understand why one person's food is another person's poison. Some blood types handle grains better than animal proteins and fat. My blood type is well equipped to digest and metabolize animal proteins and fats, but it doesn't process some grains very well. I had long noticed that I tended to gain weight when my diet included more wheat. It turned out that wheat was more easily converted into body fats and triglycerides for my type. Wheat also contains lectins with characteristics close to my blood type antigen, which could cause inflammation.

Sometimes a simple diet adjustment could bring profound health impact. A friend of mine has suffered from Hashimoto's Thyroiditis for many years. It's a disorder in which the immune system turns against the body's own tissues. Recently she went on a gluten free diet following a dietitian's recommendation. The single diet adjustment has changed her life. In a few months, her doctor informed her that she needed less dosage of medicine. The little bumps on her arms also disappeared. Apparently, gluten had acted as a trigger for her immune system malfunctions.

Luckily, although not adhering to all details, I had intuitively followed the right kind of diet for my blood type, which primarily included vegetables, fruits, rice, meat, poultries, seafood, but with very limited wheat and dairy products. All I needed were some conscious refinements.

I was more careful with the carbs intake. I identified the foods that didn't work well for me in addition to wheat and most dairy products. I either eliminated them from my diet or limited them to a minimal amount. Meanwhile, I also tried to diversify my food choices to include more beneficial or neutral foods for my type, such as expanding grain choices to quinoa, millet and other healthy varieties.

Of course, there are times I make exceptions following my "pleasure" principle. My mom is very good at making wheat based foods, such as Chinese pancakes, breads and dumplings. I love mom's foods not only because they are tasty, also because they are made with love. Yes, I gain some weight when mom comes to visit me, but who wouldn't? The solution is to trim it off immediately once mom is gone. Again, it's all about balance.

On the metabolic type analysis, there are multiple versions on the market. I primarily looked at information online and used it as a secondary reference after blood type analysis. In general, there are three metabolic types, Protein Type, Carbo Type and Mixed Type.

Protein type people, like me, burn proteins and fats much more efficiently than they burn carbs; they are more suited for a diet of high protein, moderate fat and less carbs. Carbo type people, conversely, burn carbs more efficiently; they do better on a high-carb, low-fat, relatively low-protein diet. Of course, they should always get carbs from healthy sources such as whole grains, fruits and vegetables.

Just as one person's food is the other person's poison, the food that keeps one person trim may make another person heavier. As a personal observation, the popular high protein diet, as a weight loss approach, works very effectively for some but not for all. It may help your weight loss as well as your health when you align your diet with your unique physical characteristics.

Some other interesting facts about the metabolic types are: Protein type craves salty food, while Carbo type craves sweet food; Protein type tends to experience fatigue, while Carbo type tends to experience more stress; Protein type has a strong appetite, while Carbo type has a smaller appetite. The part about cravings really speaks to me. Although I enjoy some fine candies and desserts, I have never had cravings for sweets. I used to think it was because I was a disciplined person, but now I understand there is a biological reason behind it.

Just as mind impacts body, body also impacts mind. Cravings and psychological issues sometimes have underlying physical reasons. Craving for heavy starchy food may be related to metabolism issues resulted from a high glycemic diet—the diet that causes higher and faster rise in blood sugar and insulin levels. Psychological issues, in some cases, have a strong linkage with nutrition deficiency, such as deficiency in vitamin D, Vitamin B complex, Omega-3 fatty acids and probiotics. Recognizing such root causes is instrumental to improve both our physical and psychological conditions.

For people with certain medical conditions or genetic risks, they can further personalize their diet to address the conditions or risks. People with diabetes or with a high genetic risk of getting diabetes can benefit greatly from low glycemic diet, which causes a lower and slower rise in blood sugar and therefore insulin levels. As the ancient Greek physician Hippocrates said, "Let food be thy medicine and medicine be thy food."

As technology advances, it's possible that in the future, we won't need to refer to any of these diet plans or physical type analyses. Instead, we may be able to select a precisely personalized diet and nutrition plan based on an in-depth understanding of our genetics. If you are interested, you may search "Nutritional Genomics" online, which is an emerging science that studies the relationship between human genome, nutrition and health.

Be in Tune with Your Own Body

The second diet principle is to be self-aware and ask yourself what feels good to your body. In a world with an overwhelming amount of healthy lifestyle advice, ever-changing and often conflicting health trends, it's not enough, and can even be dangerous, to blindly follow a diet formula without first listening to our bodies.

As you experiment with different foods and diets, you may ask yourself these questions to get more in tune with your body:

- What foods make you feel more energetic or tired?
- What foods make you feel lighter or heavier?
- What foods make your stomach feel good or bad?
- What foods make you sleep better or worse?
- What foods trigger allergic reactions in you, even mild reactions?

Here are a few examples of my own observations and actions. My stomach doesn't feel good when I have ice water with a heavy meal. Therefore, I request either water with no ice or hot water with lemon to go with my meal. A heavy starchy meal always makes me tired. Therefore, I try to avoid this kind of meal as much as I can. Although both coffee and tea contain caffeine, I seem to have stronger reactions to coffee. Therefore, I choose to drink tea as my daily routine and enjoy coffee as an occasional indulgence.

As always, don't get hung up on eating right, but focus on eating right for you.

Focus on the Quality of Foods

The third diet principle is to focus on the quality of foods. Over the years, I have increasingly appreciated the quality in everything. Quality, instead of quantity, gives the most authentic and long-lasting pleasure.

The quality of food is especially important from both health and pleasure perspectives. To me, there are two aspects in high quality food, which often go hand in hand. From a health perspective, high quality foods are fresh, organic and whole. From a pleasure perspective, high quality foods are tasty in a healthy way.

High quality foods are essential in healthy living, no matter what our physical characteristics are. Low quality foods, such as processed foods, are low in nutritional value and high in substances that are not natural to the body. They can disrupt the body's normal cellular function and metabolism, cause weight gain even with moderate calories, and are root causes for many chronic degenerative diseases.

Nutrition and Physical Degeneration, a classic book written by Dr. Weston A. Price, has been my most inspirational source so far regarding the quality of food. Dr. Price, a Cleveland dentist who was called the "Isaac Newton of Nutrition," traveled the world to study the factors responsible for the fine teeth among the primitives in different parts of the world, such as isolated villages in Switzerland, Inuits in Alaska, and Indians of North America.

In contrast to modern societies, the primitives were healthy physically, stable emotionally and free from degenerative diseases. Based on his study, he concluded that modern dental problems, as well as health problems, were signs of physical degeneration resulting from nutritional deficiencies.

The primitives of different areas had tremendously different food structures, which often didn't follow the "standard" healthy diet prescribed today. The main food sources of the Alaskan Inuits were sea foods such as fish, walrus, seal, marine mammals and organs. 90% of their diet was composed of protein and fat, with only small amounts of nuts, berries and vegetables. The main food sources of Melanesians on the Fiji Islands were plant foods & vegetables, fruit, coconuts, coconut oil, shellfish and fish. Yet, they all lived healthy lives.

In spite of their different food sources, what's common about the primitive's food was its high quality. They were gifts of nature, organic, unprocessed and rich in essential nutrients. Their food provided many times more vitamins and minerals than our modern devitalized food, which is nutritionally depleted and loaded with chemical fertilizers and hormones.

As the Chinese saying wisely offers, "One area of water and soil raises one area of people." God has amazing ways to feed people. Although Inuits had limited amounts of fruits and vegetables, certain layers of the whale's skin were very high in vitamin C and seal oil was one of the richest foods in vitamin A. As Dr. Price humbly wrote, "Our world, our food and our lives have potentials so vast that we can only observe directions, not goals... Yes, man's place is most exalted when he obeys Mother Nature's laws."

In addition to its practical value, food is also a main source of pleasure in life. Although it has become a source of guilt for many people, it's natural and healthy to seek pleasure in food. Fresh fruits and vegetables can bring more immediate joy than any material gift.

When I was a child, my friends and I loved to play on their family farm lands. In summer, we would pick the fully ripened watermelons, tomatoes, cucumbers, and enjoy them right off the vines. Sometimes at dinner, we had a difficult time eating what we were served at the table, because we had gorged ourselves during the day.

Being someone very open-minded about food, I feel that almost any type of food has the potential to be both healthy and tasty, when made with finest ingredients, techniques and care.

I have never considered hamburger a healthy food until I visited a hamburger restaurant specializing in super fresh and organic ingredients. My children didn't like Chinese food until they visited Hong Kong and South China. The food there was characterized by fresh ingredients, delicate preparation and high variety. They loved it so much that they looked forward to every meal.

When a friend of mine arrived in the U.S., she was shocked to observe that the country seemed to be primarily a "fast food nation," obsessed with drive-through, low-cost convenience. She told me that she didn't like American food. After she met a boyfriend, who happened to be a food connoisseur, she came to me and said, "I never thought American food could be so healthy and tasty!"

Several years ago, I came across a quaint candy store when I looked for a Christmas present. Their elegant handmade candies once received the "Best of Chicago" award. I loved a particular candy called "Tizzy Lizzy," made from white chocolate, cranberries, almond toffee bits, pretzels, and light coconut; drizzled with caramel and dark chocolate.

The owner, Marilyn, was a warm and joyful lady. She had been passionate about candy making all her life. We once talked about the recipe for "Tizzy Lizzy." She said she had shared the recipe with some customers, but no one had been able to duplicate the taste. I was quite curious and asked why. She told me that the secret was in the ingredients. She sourced the finest ingredients from all over the world. There was no way the ingredients from grocery stores could match that. I thanked her for a great lesson on quality.

High quality food is worth investing in for both health and pleasure purposes. As we develop a taste for quality, we naturally need less in quantity. A few pieces of fine candies from Marilyn were enough to keep me away from all the other mediocre candies displayed by the bagful, beckoning us at the checkout counter.

If your budget is limited, you can save money by eliminating the many unhealthy snacks, drinks, and opting for fewer, organic, whole foods. Instead of frequenting nutrition-poor fast food restaurants, you can celebrate a few special events with family and friends at healthier restaurants. Don't get into the rut of meal time being like a "pit stop" at an auto race. The words "fast food," may result in overly "fat food."

You have a solid foundation for optimum health when your diet is tailored to your own physical characteristics and involves high quality food. However, food alone may not be enough to fulfill our nutrition need in today's changing world.

12

Nutritional Supplementation: When Food Is Not Enough

> The doctor of the future will no longer treat the human frame with drugs, but rather will cure and prevent disease with nutrition.
> —*Thomas Edison*

I considered myself a healthy eater compared to most of the population. Being someone who preferred everything to be natural, I was against anything that didn't seem "natural," including nutritional supplements. I used to believe that food alone was enough to fulfill my nutrition needs, and I felt sorry for the people who picked up vitamin bottles stacked on the shelves of supermarkets and health food stores.

It wasn't until I experienced a sub-health condition that I seriously looked into my nutrition reality. I began to suspect that I might have some nutrition deficiency, which was compounded by two childbirths.

Although I had been committed to high quality food as much as I could, I must admit that I ate out more frequently than I would have preferred. Given my busy lifestyle, it was simply impossible to cook a nutritionally complete and balanced meal every day, like the meals I had during my health and education retreat in Mexico. Each meal there was moderate in size but involved a large variety of healthy food ingredients.

I also realized that our environment had changed dramatically. Even the "organic food" was not the same as the "organic food" I enjoyed when I was a child. I could optimize my micro environment at home as much as possible, but I couldn't escape the macro environment in which we all live.

When I came to the United States in 1998, the word "big" constantly came to my mind. The land was big, the houses were big, and even the vegetables were big. The first time I stepped into a grocery store, I was amazed by the big, beautifully shaped green peppers and tomatoes, because the vegetables in China were smaller, sometimes irregularly shaped and with worm holes. However, I noticed that these beautiful-looking vegetables were not as tasty as those vegetables we had in China. Whether cooked, or eaten raw, they lacked the deep, rich flavors.

As my nutritional research continued, I made the connection between the lack of flavors in food and the nutrition depletion in food, and I was shocked by the severity of nutrition depletion in our soil and in our food.

The 1992 Rio Earth Summit, a United Nation conference on world environment, concluded there had been severe and continuing mineral declines in the soils throughout the world. Over the last 100 years, average mineral levels in agricultural soils had fallen by 85% in North America, 76% in Asia, and 72% in Europe.

According to the Nutrition Security Institute, a non-profit organization concerned with the fertility of the soil, the nutrition in our food had declined tremendously over the 80 years. The major micro nutrients in an apple declined almost 80% over 80 years. It means that we need to eat five apples today to equal the nutrition that our ancestors received from one apple. The problem is, we don't have a stomach a few times larger than our ancestors.

The nutrition depletion in food was also observed by the government. Back to 1977, Dr. Walter Mertz from the U.S. Department of Agriculture made this statement to congress, "In the future, we will not be able to rely on a balanced diet to provide the essential trace elements because such a diet will be very difficult to obtain."

To illustrate Dr. Mertz's point, today, if we want to receive 400 IU of vitamin E, which is the optimum daily intake recommended by nutrition experts, we need to eat 20 pounds of spinach, or 2 pounds of almonds. Again, we don't have a stomach big enough to contain this amount of food, nor would we want to eat in such quantities.

As the micro nutrients have become increasingly depleted, there has been a rapid increase in chronic degenerative diseases, such as cancer, diabetes and heart disease. Dr. Bernard Jensen, author of the book *Empty Harvest*, stated, "The immunity of the human body is parallel with the immunity of the soil." Dr. Linus Pauling, two-time Nobel Prize winner, once said, "You can trace every sickness, every disease and every ailment to a mineral deficiency."

The severe nutrition deletion in foods is caused by nutrition depletion in soil. It is also caused by technologies, such as modern farming methods; picking, storage and transportation technologies; and food processing technologies.

Today people in certain regions of the world may still be able to get enough nutrition from food, especially in non-industrialized areas where people continue to live a traditional lifestyle. However, it's virtually impossible for average Americans to get enough nutrition from food alone. It's a reality that we all have to face, even for someone like me, who would rather to have everything natural whenever possible.

In 2002, the Journal of the American Medical Association (JAMA) reversed its long standing anti-supplement position and published two scientific reviews which acknowledged that it's prudent for all adults to take supplements.

Again, Quality Is the Key

As I accepted that nutritional supplementation was necessary, I also became aware of the staggering amount of conflicting opinions about nutritional supplements, ranging from being harmful, to being useless, and to being beneficial. I was committed to separate the myths from the truths for the benefit of my own health. Here are a few things that I have learned from my investigation.

The quality of the supplements, from ingredients, manufacturing to formulation, makes a world of difference. To make a generalized statement based on one brand or one product is logically problematic as products of different qualities could lead to completely different results. I have experienced the difference personally after trying products of both the lowest and the highest ratings.

As a side note, you should always be alert when you hear any over generalized opinion because most likely it is inaccurate, such as "all men are the same," as my friend always complained.

Most of us understand that ingredients and manufacturing make a difference, but are less aware of the difference made by formulation. Vitamin E works differently when it's supplemented alone and when it is taken together with other complete and balanced nutrients. Many misleading studies have been based upon results from supplementing a single nutrient and then trying to observe its impact in isolation. They failed to recognize the fact that the body is a sophisticated biochemistry factory and no nutrient works in isolation.

It can be a daunting task to choose the right supplement from over a thousand brands. In 1994, Congress passed a law called the Dietary Supplement Health and Education Act. The law limited FDA's ability to regulate the industry. Research indicated that half of the supplements on the market couldn't be properly absorbed by the body and one third of the products had contents not matching what was displayed on the label. It's no surprise that supplement scandals constantly appear in the media, even including brands sold by reputable retailers.

To ensure a supplement is truly safe and effective, it's important to choose products manufactured against pharmaceutical Good Manufacturing Practices (GMP) and products that meet the USP standard. These two standards help ensure that what's on the label matches the content, and that the product can properly break down and be absorbed by the body.

It's also wise to look for brands with approvals from authoritative third-party organizations such as NSF and ConsumerLab. Brands certified for sports and used by active world class athletes are also good choices, because athletes demand a much higher safety level in terms of substances and performance. As you choose your supplements, always aim for the highest quality products you can find. Mediocre products offer limited benefits, and some of them may indeed bring more harms than benefits.

When you research nutritional supplements, you want to be careful about the overwhelming amount of opinions on the Internet or social media. Virtually anything can be said on the Internet today, good or bad, right or wrong, with credible references or not. It's important to seek counsel from authoritative sources and qualified professionals.

Nutrition is a field different from the traditional medical disciplines. Most of the doctors in the United States and in China have received limited nutritional training. We should always consult physicians regarding the use of supplements during medical treatments, but our general practitioners may not be well-informed when it comes to nutritional supplementation. Just as we would not seek cancer advice from a cardiologist, we would be better served to seek nutrition counsel from a professional specializing in nutrition.

Your Personalized Supplementation Program

Many of us automatically think of vitamins when it comes to nutritional supplements, but supplements go far beyond vitamins. The basic micro nutrient supplement, sometimes called essential nutrients, support the body's overall health. A quality product should include complete and balanced micro nutrients including vitamins, minerals, wide spectrum antioxidants and other nutrients that support various cell and body functions; it is much more than a "multi-vitamin" pill with only a few vitamins or minerals assembled together.

In addition, some supplements support special needs such as mother and child health, weight management or detoxification. Some supplements, sometimes called optimizers, support the health of specific body systems, such as our cardiovascular system or skeletal system.

We can design a personalized nutritional supplementation program that is tailored to our specific health goals and priorities, through a strategic mix of essential nutrients, optimizers, and other supplements supporting special needs.

As a starting point, we want to ensure that our digestive system functions effectively. A healthy digestive system is the foundation for overall health. Without a well-functioning digestive system, we can't absorb and utilize the nutrients effectively, no matter how good our diet and nutrition programs are. Just as we want to prime the wall before we paint it, we want to improve our digestive and detox functions and prime the body before adding other supplements.

We can then supply the body with complete and balanced essential nutrients. Also, we can add optimizers to strengthen the functions that are our health weak spots or our high genetic risk areas. Someone concerned with cardiovascular health may want to add optimizers that enhance cardiovascular functions, such as omega-3 fatty acids and CoQ10. Someone with a family history of osteoporosis may want to add optimizers that enhance the bone health, such as calcium, magnesium, and vitamin D.

A personalized nutritional supplementation program helps improve our overall health, strengthen specific body functions, and restore the body's balance and harmony. It may also serve as a complementary treatment and help address the root causes of some health problems.

However, it's critical to recognize that nutritional supplements are NOT medicine. They are intended to help us become healthier but not intended to cure specific diseases. We should be cautious about any advertisements or statements claiming that some nutritional supplements can cure diseases.

It takes a long time for the body to grow out of balance. It also takes a long time to restore that balance and not all the damages can be reversed. When a disease arises, we want to immediately seek medical treatments from qualified physicians. The longer we delay, the more serious the conditions may become, to a point where they may be difficult to cure.

If you are taking prescription or over-the-counter medicines or going through medical treatments, you should always inform your doctor about the supplements you use, because there may be potential conflicts between the medicines and the supplements. If you are on a regimen of high dosage blood thinners, you should be cautious with supplements containing omega-3 fish oil as this could result in your blood becoming too thin.

My Health Transformation

To address my sub-health condition, I conducted my own investigation into the world of nutritional supplements, and ultimately decided to go for a pharmaceutical grade nutritional supplementation program, with which I felt comfortable from a quality and safety perspective.

I began with a digestion and detox program composed of probiotic, digestive enzyme, fiber and a product supporting liver health. After that, I began the micro nutrients supplementation which included complete and balanced essential nutrients, and optimizers such as grape seed extract, calcium and magnesium.

To my disbelief, my sub-health condition started to improve within two weeks. Gradually, my energy was back. My runny nose in the morning disappeared. I used to catch a cold every winter and cough for at least one month. However, I passed that winter comfortably without getting sick. On a summer day, I attended a meeting at which a lady complained about the freezing air conditioning, even with her cardigan sweater on. A few others echoed her sentiment. I suddenly realized that, instead of joining the protest, I didn't feel cold and I was not even wearing a sweater!

In addition to the improvement in my overall health, I enjoyed an unexpected bonus. I found it easier to control my weight. I was blessed with my parent's genes, resulting in me being relatively thin. When I was younger, I could pretty much eat anything without gaining weight. However, my metabolism slowed down as I grew older. If I had a big dinner, I needed to balance it out with fruit and veggie based lunch for the next few days. After getting on my supplementation program, I found that it only took me a day or two to balance out a big dinner instead of a few days. Because my digestive system and my metabolism worked more effectively, I even lost some weight over the next few months.

Many of us are probably more concerned about weight than other aspects of health. Although weight problems are commonly attributed to overeating and a lack of physical activities, there are many other reasons for weight gain such as low quality food, improper diet structure, bacterial imbalance, digestive problems, micro nutrients deficiency, and insulin resistance. A friend of mine lost fifteen pounds after changing to a low glycemic diet and getting on a supplementation program. Another friend lost five pounds simply by improving digestive functions.

As I have observed, many people are not able to lose weight simply by increasing exercise or starving themselves. Even if they do have dramatic results, with what we call "the yo-yo diet syndrome," the former weight almost always returns, because the underlying root causes are not addressed.

We may or may not be able to pinpoint what exactly causes our weight problems. However, it's always a good practice to eliminate common causes first, such as ensuring your diet structure is proper, your digestive system is functioning properly and your micro nutrients are complete and balanced.

Our changing environments and lifestyles require us to take a dynamic, ever-evolving approach to health and well-being. Even if you believe you have excellent food selection in your daily diet, as I used to believe, you may be surprised by the positive benefits of a high quality, personalized nutritional supplementation regimen.

13

Your Exercise, Your Day

Those who do not find time for exercise, will have to find
time for illness.
—*Edward Stanley*

Our bodies rarely "wear out" from activity, as a result of
work or recreation. However, many people literally "rust
out" due to inactivity and a sedentary lifestyle. Especially
today, as technology replaces physical exertion, we need to
get up and get out of that easy chair. The body was not
designed to sit and stare. It was designed to move, walk,
play, run, stroll, hike, swim and dance!

Exercise offers many benefits, such as better health, a
slimmer shape and a more fitted look. Just as our dietary
and nutritional needs are individual and personal, the
subject of exercise is extremely personal too. One approach
definitely does not fit for all.

A friend of mine bought an annual membership in a
gym because people around her exercised there, but she
didn't like to go to gym and rarely used her membership
pass. She felt guilty about her lack of willpower, and
grumbled from time to time, "I should go to the gym
tomorrow... I really should go... I must go." I couldn't help

asking her, "Why do you have to go to gym if it's so difficult for you?"

I was amused and nodded in agreement, when I came across a little poem online, written by Dorothy Heller:

I spent a fortune on a trampoline,
A stationary bike, and a rowing machine;
Complete with gadgets to read my pulse,
And gadgets to prove my progress results.
And others to show the miles I've charted,
But they left off the gadget to get me started!

Many of us, like my friend, follow others or the popular trends when it comes to exercise. We allow outside voices to dictate how we should exercise, instead of listening to our own body and considering what's natural and fun for us as individuals. As a result, it's difficult for us to get motivated and sustain whatever exercise routine we pursue.

My personal exercise program is by no means the best, but simply something that has worked for my unique situations. It is meant to urge you to listen to your own inner voice, and design a personal exercise program working for you.

Tailor Your Exercise Program to Fit Yourself

A well-rounded exercise program should ideally encompass four types of exercise: cardio, strength, balance, and flexibility. Each type of exercise offers unique benefits, while all of them improve our overall health. Although each type of exercise is defined separately, some exercises cover multiple types and can serve multiple purposes. Yoga is both a flexibility exercise and a balance exercise. Running is both a cardio exercise and a strength exercise.

As a busy working mom, I had a few considerations when I chose my exercises. First, I prefer exercises that cover multiple types and serve multiple purposes. This way I can maximize the benefits within my limited time.

Second, I prefer exercises that are convenient and can be easily incorporated into my daily routines, such as body-only exercises, or exercises I can do with simple equipment at home. I don't go to outside gyms other than occasionally participating in group lessons at my office gym. I would rather save the time involved in commuting to an outside facility at inconvenient times of the day, especially with young children at home.

Third, I prefer exercises that are simple. Fitness regimens requiring sophisticated bodily/kinesthetic skills don't motivate me, because I am not endowed with these natural talents.

Last, I prefer exercises that I can enjoy. Moderation and sustainability are important to me. If I must force myself to exercise by sheer willpower, it's not going to be sustainable. I tried several intense workouts in the past but was not able to stick to them. I noticed how rapidly I became out of shape again once I stopped. I have avoided these workouts in spite of their great benefits because I know myself well enough not to rely on my willpower again.

Based on these considerations, I chose several exercises as part of my personal exercise program: walking, rebounding, rope jumping, yoga, some plank exercises and crunches.

I walk whenever possible. I walk after lunch around the lake by my office. I walk after dinner in my neighborhood park as I watch children play. I walk across parking lots, rather than look for the most convenient parking spots. I walk up and down stairs, unless I am in a high-rise building. It is ironically amusing to see people take an escalator to the second floor, where their workout center is located.

In summer months, I like to jump rope or jump on my rebounder in the backyard with my children. You most likely are familiar with rebounders, which are small, round, trampolines. Rebounding is not a highly popular exercise today. However, as I learned from my health and education retreat in Mexico, it is actually one of the best exercises. It gives a whole-body workout and can cover all four types of exercises with the many different ways you can rebound. It strengthens muscles and bones, improves balance, stimulates lymphatic system and facilitates the body's natural detoxification. It is twice as effective as running but without the extra stress on joints.

I also love the two jumping exercises for stress relief purpose. I don't get overly stressed often, but when I do, the physical symptoms, such as shortness of breath and insomnia, can last for several days. In the past, I used to relieve stress by spending quiet time by myself, listening to music or walking. It helped me relax mentally, but it would still take a long time to get rid of the physical symptoms.

As I studied blood type analysis, I learned that intense exercise relieves stress most effectively for my blood type, while quiet, relaxation techniques, such as yoga or meditation, work more effectively for other blood types.

On one stressful summer day, I decided to test out this new stress relief technique while enjoying the beautiful sunny sky and the smell of our freshly cut lawn. For thirty minutes, I took turns jumping on the rebounder and then alternating with the jump rope. I was sweating and tired, but my stress symptoms were almost all gone by evening!

In addition to my basic exercise program, I do other exercises sporadically as time allows, such as dancing, aerobics, or helping my children with volleyball and badminton practice. Surprisingly, playing sports at my children's level is quite enjoyable for me. Because we play at a slower pace, my lack of aptitude doesn't seem to be a problem.

The one theme behind all these exercises is: do what is comfortable and natural for you.

The Myths About Exercise

Just as there are many myths concerning nutritional supplements, there are a lot of myths regarding fitness and exercise. I have often encountered two of these myths. One is that exercise is sufficient to keep one healthy; one doesn't need to pay attention to diet and nutrition if he or she exercises regularly and intensely.

The truth is, every aspect of our lifestyles plays a unique and important role in our health. They must be coordinated and balanced as a chain is only as strong as its weakest link. A person who rarely moves is unlikely to be healthy no matter how well he eats, and similarly, a person with nutrition deficiency is unlikely to be healthy no matter how often he works out. With bricks and lumber missing, we can't make a solid building no matter how hard we hammer the rest of the structure.

Intense exercises create more free radicals and oxidative stress, which actually speed up the body's aging process. That's why athletes engaged in intensive trainings are the very people who need the best nutrition, particularly wide spectrum antioxidants, to counter the negative effects of oxidative stress.

The second myth is that, as a society, we are exercising more and becoming more fit with the mind-boggling variety of fitness trends flooding the market.

After a 10-year study, the Centers for Disease Control in Atlanta reports that only 8% of adults, age 18-65 do any regular exercise, meaning 20 minutes or more of vigorous exercise, 3 or more times per week. Couch-potato-ism is on a roll, even among the young and presumably vigorous. The latest survey of students in all 50 states shows that only 37% do any regular exercise. That's an incredible decline from the 62% that exercised regularly in the 1980's and the 50% that worked out in the 1990's.

As a society, we are getting wider instead of leaner every year. During the past several decades, the average weight of women aged 18-74 has increased by 4 pounds, and the average weight of men in the same age range has increased by 6 pounds. And according to recent studies released by the National Institutes of Health, young adults are being impacted the most. Men and women in the 20-30 age group are now 10 pounds heavier than the same age group was in 1996. While the largest population group in the world today carries the label "baby boomers," it would be tragic if a generation in the near future carries the label of "baby blubbers," as one friend named it.

I can't help wondering: What has been missing in our exercise picture? Why do people exercise much less now compared to the past, in spite of the myriad of exercise options? Why do people in under-industrialized countries remain fit even without the sophisticated, high-tech fitness craze sweeping this country?

Exercise used to be an easy, natural and integral part of everyday life. It still is in certain under-industrialized countries. People exercised through their daily chores such as harvesting food, housework, running errands and walking to work and school.

Now, however, in spite of the great benefits the fitness industry offers, exercise has become burdensome for many people. It is hard, artificial work isolated from the other parts of life, and another "scheduled" project to be squeezed into an already crowded calendar.

It's not surprising why so many of us struggle with exercise today. If you happen to be struggling too, you may want to take a fresh look at your exercise approach. Use common sense, be creative, and develop an exercise program that is natural, easy and comfortable for you.

Follow Your Biological Clock

For each of us, there seem to be time periods in which our energy levels peak and ebb, according to our individual biological clocks. The biological clock plays a vital role in our health. In addition to sleep cycles, it affects nearly all biological functions in our body, such as digestion, blood pressure, and the function of different organs. It can even be found at the cellular level. Most of us are aware of our biological clock type to a certain degree. Using birds as a metaphor, we may be larks or early birds, who go to sleep early and wake up early; owls or late birds, who like to stay up very late; or hummingbirds, who can go either way.

As a working mom, with little free time, I try to utilize my time thoughtfully. I made conscious lifestyle adjustments once I became aware of my biological clock.

I rarely stay up late as I am not able to sleep well if I go to bed after a certain hour. Occasionally, when there was an urgent project, I was tempted to stay up late to finish it. When I did that, I always regretted it. I lost focus as the hours progressed, and my lack of sleep resulted in me feeling tired the entire next day.

I used to think of it as a matter of my lacking stamina, until I recognized that I was a typical lark. I began to relax more during the evening, mostly just doing light activities with my family. After getting up in the morning, instead of lounging around, I would work on productive activities.

I also found ways to better utilize time during the day when I am most energetic. My car became "a rolling university," as I listened to educational programs during my commute between work and home. I also tried to make most of my personal phone calls during my walking exercise and during my children's extracurricular activities.

There are several other interesting facts about biological clock types. Unlike owls, larks are less likely to sleep in during their days off. As a lark, I woke up early during the weekends as I did during the weekdays. I used to feel frustrated that I never had the luxury of sleeping in as others do. I now understand the reason. A lark's mood declines slightly throughout the day while an owl's mood rises substantially as the day progresses. Therefore, larks like me are better working on day jobs. Owls work better on evening shifts and tolerate rotating shifts better. Not surprisingly, most of the ER doctors are owls.

Certain medicines and treatments, such as chemotherapy, work more effectively at certain times of the day depending on an individual's biological clock. Chronotherapy is a way of treating disease or illness that strategically works with our biological clock and takes advantage of the body's natural rhythms and cycles. It can be helpful in boosting the positive results of our medical treatment.

Take Charge of Your Health, Beginning Today

My health has gone full circle since I followed my personalized healthy lifestyle. Not only did I say farewell to the sub-health condition, I now feel younger and more energetic than I did a few years ago. I am more confident to take care of my loved ones as well as to pursue my dreams in life.

Lifestyle choices make remarkable differences as we age. At fifty years of age, one woman appears and functions as young and energetic as a typical forty-year-old, and another woman already looks and functions as a typical sixty-year-old. At eighty years of age, one man resides in a nursing home or hospital bed enduring pain and suffering, and another man still travels the world and enjoys the golden years.

It is difficult for people to imagine aging as it is to imagine death. Therefore, we often make poor lifestyle choices until it's too late. If you are brave and courageous, search "how I look like when I am old" online, you may get a brand-new perspective on how to enhance your daily life.

Good health cannot and must not be taken for granted. It should be a top priority, given our full attention, in every day of our lives. Only by maintaining good health can we do what we need to do and want to do. Most of us work hard to save money and look forward to relishing the golden years after retirement. Only later do we discover that we are going to spend a great deal of money and effort trying to regain the health we sacrificed during our earlier years.

Take charge of your health from this day forward. Don't wait until your body complains. It is your one and only transportation vehicle for your entire life journey. Treat it as the spacecraft it was designed to be. Maintain and fine tune it every day.

14

Projecting Your Unique Style

In order to be irreplaceable one must always be different.
—Coco Chanel

Some of our physical characteristics impact our health. Some of them impact our appearance, such as our facial structure, body shape, skin color and eye color. These physical characteristics that make up our appearance are in our "nature." However, our appearance also very much depends on how we positively "nurture" and accentuate our "nature."

The Years of Style Mishaps

Our appearance is the first thing we present to the world. It can either boost or hinder our self-confidence and self-esteem. In my childhood in China, parents and teachers emphasized that we should pay the least amount of attention to our appearance in order not to be distracted from our duties as a student. As a bookworm child, I was fine with that idea. Except for a few sporadic rebellions, I happily wore whatever my parents handed me to wear.

When I advanced into college, I had to buy clothes for myself. To be honest, shopping was not a pleasant experience for me. Because I had no idea what to buy, the easiest choice was to copy what was popular on campus. It seemed to be what a lot of people did anyway. I was not sure about the others, but the questions like "Does this color, shape, style work for me?" never entered my mind.

I did realize, however, that I didn't look good in most of the clothing that was worn by the more stylish girls. The colorful, elaborately decorated dresses looked stunning on that tall, fashionable girl. The "hello kitty" T-shirt looked very cute on that dainty, sweet girl. But once I put them on, I somehow looked silly.

I had trouble with my hair as well. I had no idea what hair style looked good for me. I walked into a different hair salon and picked a different style each time, hoping that this particular day would be my lucky day. Unfortunately, the days mostly turned out to be unlucky.

On one occasion, a honey-tongued hair stylist persuaded me to perm my hair. It was my first perm and it was a total disaster. I was devastated when I saw myself in the mirror, looking like a forty-year-old matron with short, big hair exploded with small curls. It was as if I had put my finger into an electrical outlet, and the current had shocked me especially in my hair! I had met my future husband not long before that experience. I still remember his horrified reaction when he saw my new look.

As I moved on from college into the work place, things got a little bit better. The office dress codes were more conservative and professional, which was great for me because I had fewer choices to deal with. Somehow, I looked better in those conservative clothes.

After we moved to the United States, though, a new set of challenges arose. I was overwhelmed by the size of the shopping malls and by the sheer volume of clothing sized much larger than my frame. Back then I was a size oo in today's sizing terms and it was challenging to find clothing that fit me. Once again, I was lost in the shopping game.

In the first two years in the U.S., I ended up wearing clothes either larger or poorly fitting. The few skirts and pants that fit in the waist were far oversized for my hips. Over the years, I randomly found some stores that catered to my size, but these stores were not available everywhere in the country. As I moved several times, shopping generally became a haphazard experience.

Style Is More Than a Fashion Statement

In my younger years, I found certain comfort in what my parents and teachers preached to me as a child: "Your look is not important. It is your academic and work performance that counts." They, of course, had a valid point. Worthiness should be based more on the valuable contribution we make to the world through our service and dedication. And, yes, popular culture seems to feature style over substance, and skin-deep celebrity over intrinsic integrity. However, there needs to be a balance between style and substance in our choices.

As I grew older, I began to re-evaluate what I had learned as a child. As much as we shouldn't judge anyone by his or her appearance, we are judged by our appearance, whether we like it or not, and whether it is fair or not. I used to feel indignant about how "shallow" people and society were to judge by appearance. But I later learned that this was a natural part of human psychology.

Research has indicated that we only get a few seconds to make a first impression, and that first impression will largely influence the future of a relationship. As it's said, first impression can last a lifetime and we never get a second chance for a first impression.

Our outward appearances and actions, such as our image, style, body language, cleanliness and neatness, tell an immediate story about the content inside. A polished and confident look indicates a sense of control and good self-management in life. It invites others to learn more about our content.

There is a critical difference in having a style that mimics current fads and tries to please others, and one that makes us confident and comfortable in our own skin. Some women, and even teenage girls, fall into the trap of constantly being self-conscious about their look. They are somewhat obsessed as to whether their look emulates the current fashion trends or attracts romantic partners. Pleasing others takes priority over expressing their own potential.

A style that is clean, polished and expresses our unique self is distinctly different. It brings out the best of our unique features, makes us comfortable and confident in who we are, and helps us project optimism concerning our potential.

A poor style limits the extent to which our content can be recognized and our potential can be developed. Our style influences how we are viewed in the workplace and how we are treated in life, from simple restaurant experiences to significant matters of the heart. After I was admitted into the MBA program, our school held an orientation session. Early in the presentation the speaker stressed the importance of dressing for success. There are exceptions, but in general, people successful in life do look more polished.

An inadequate sense of style is also a major source of closet waste. The dusty clothes that used to be in my closet could testify to that. Because I didn't know what styles worked for me, I kept buying and continued to "have nothing to wear."

The U.S. has long been labeled as one of the biggest waste-generating countries. This was not surprising as we looked at the overflowing stuff in the average American household, with women's clothing being a major part of it. I needed only to look in my own closet to see how I had become a waste-generating "consumer."

I have been attracted to the idea of "zero waste" as part of the minimalist living concept. The good news is, it's possible to look stylish and achieve zero waste, or minimal waste, at the same time. I once read an article titled "French women only need nine pieces of clothing." This may be an overstatement, but French women do manage to look stylish with a smaller closet.

When I visited Paris, I stayed at a French woman artist's apartment located right by the Champs-Élysées. It was a beautiful, decent-sized apartment. There was a huge built-in floor to ceiling bookshelf along the extended hallway; among the French books was a fascinating collection of charming, old English books. The closet, however, was surprisingly small. I remembered saying to myself, "Maybe the contrast between the bookshelf and the closet is another style secret of French women?"

My Style Transformation Begins

I was determined to change my look after the moment of awakening during my maternity leave. I wanted to find my own unique style and I wanted to have zero waste in my closet. Even more, I wanted to be a role model for my daughters, so that they would not need to endure the trial and error phases and repeat the mistakes I had made for more than thirty years.

As I studied the many aspects of personal style, I became aware of my unique physical features, and the styles and brands working best for these features. I learned wardrobe planning techniques and thoroughly revamped my closet. It felt like a new world was opening up before me. In the past, everything about my physical features seemed to be a projection of liabilities that worked against me. As I learned and changed, I started to see assets, as well as opportunities to turn my perceived liabilities into assets.

Some of you may have been inherently blessed with a good sense of style, or may have been trained as a child about a good sense of style. Others, like me, may have to devote a lot of time and energy to acquire it later in life. The positive news is, to a great extent, learning and practice can enhance our sense of style. If you happen to be struggling with your style as I did, I hope my experience can assure you that, you can cultivate a better sense of style as long as you are willing to do your homework.

Body Shape: Find Balance and Proportion

An essential part of style is about creating the right balance and proportion, based on an understanding of our body shapes. There are different ways to look at body shapes. A common way is to view the proportion between shoulder, waist and hip, and define our body shape into four basic types: triangular, rectangular, inverted triangle, and hourglass.

Another way is to look at muscle and fat distribution, and define our body shape by one of three types: ectomorphs, mesomorphs and endomorphs. Ectomorphs are delicate with narrow frames, like Audrey Hepburn. Mesomorphs have more muscles with a thin waist, like Tina Turner. Endomorphs are feminine and curvy, like Marilyn Monroe.

Each body shape is described with a list of key characteristics, which may only partially agree with how we define ourselves. According to an online article from the U.K. newspaper *Daily Mail*, 25% of women interviewed didn't believe their figure fit into any defined body shapes. Instead of fitting myself into a type, I simply borrowed all the characteristics applicable to me and put together a list to describe my own shape. This list has been very useful to guide my style decisions.

Knowing our body shape, we can achieve an ideal balance and proportion through strategic use of shapes, patterns, fabrics, and colors. This knowledge alone led to a major wardrobe transformation.

I had pieces that always made me feel heavy and uncomfortable for reasons I couldn't explain. I was able to see why as I learned about my body shape. Some of the pieces exaggerated my already broader shoulders, such as the dress with puffy shoulders, the jacket with thick shoulder pads, and the buttoned shirt in stiff fabrics. Some of them overwhelmed my small frame, such as the loose-fitting sweater dress with big flowery patterns. These pieces were immediately placed into the "to get rid of" basket.

To balance my broader shoulders and narrow hips, it would work better for me to understate the tops and highlight the bottoms. Unfortunately, as I took inventory of my wardrobe, I found it accentuated the opposite features. I immediately adjusted my shopping approach. I began to acquire tops that were single-colored, form fitting, in soft fabrics, with simple lines and designs. Meanwhile, I began to purchase skirts and shoes of various colors and patterns. I particularly liked A-line skirts or dresses as they were very versatile.

As part of our body shape study, we also want to identify our unique assets and liabilities, highlight the assets and understate the liabilities. If you have beautiful shoulders, accentuate them with shoulderless tops. If you have well-toned arms, show them off with sleeveless dresses. If you have nicely shaped legs, by all means, feature them with short, knee-length skirts and slim pants.

You can find a wealth of information online about dressing by body shapes. A good book that I found very helpful was *The Pocket Stylist: Behind-the-Scenes Expertise from a Fashion Pro on Creating Your Own Look*, written by Kendall Farr. Some of the specific shopping tips may no longer apply, but the principles are timeless.

Colors: What is Your Season?

A good use of colors brightens our face, our eyes and makes us look young and refreshed. Conversely, a poor use of colors makes us look dull and tired. There are many different tools to help people discover the best color palette for them. If you google "color me," a long list of resources will be displayed. I personally benefited most from the four-season color approach.

I came across an old little book *Color Me Beautiful*, written by Carole Jackson. Although the pictures were far out-of-date, I was fascinated by the simple yet applicable principles. The book defined people into four color seasons: spring, summer, autumn and winter, based on skin tone, eye color and hair color. It then offered a color palette suitable for each season.

I discovered my color season as "winter," characterized by cool skin undertone, dark hair and dark eyes. Colors working best for "winter" are neutral colors such as white, black, gray, and navy; sharp and clear colors such as bright blue, emerald green, violet, turquoise; light and icy colors such as icy pink and icy blue.

Some of the colors that work the worst for "winter" are brown, orange and pastel colors. I used to own several brown and bright orange colored tops. They were expensive pieces that I bought on impulse. Although they looked beautiful on the hangers, I looked drab and tired every time I wore them.

They ended up staying on the most remote shelf of my closet. I was puzzled and frustrated, but still hoped that someday they would miraculously work with some new pieces. After learning about my color season, I came to terms with the conclusion that they would never work for me. These pieces immediately went into the "to get rid of" basket.

White is a neutral color but it can be a tricky color. Although everyone can wear white, each different color season is suited to a different shade of white. I, as a "winter" person, would do better with pure, bright white, while a "summer" person would do better with ivory white. No wonder I never wanted to wear my ivory colored shirt!

People of different color seasons can wear the same hue. The difference in their color palette is largely related to value (i.e. the degree of lightness or darkness) and chroma (i.e. the degree of saturation). White is not just white and red is not just red. The numerous variations of colors that used to overwhelm me now speak to me in a more meaningful way.

Knowing our ideal color palette empowers us to make the best color choices in clothing, makeup and accessories. Basic knowledge of color theory also gives us more discerning eyes when it comes to the various applications of colors, from personal style to interior design.

Face Shape: More Potential Than You Think

Our face shape influences a series of style choices, such as hair style, make up, jewelry and accessories. There are four basic face shapes: round, square, oval and heart.

In traditional Asian culture, oval is considered as the most beautiful face shape. I have a square, angular face with strong jaw lines. As I grew up, I had always considered my face as plain and unattractive. I never bothered to explore its potential until I made the decision to make the best out of my look.

It's easy to find everything that works best for your face shape on the Internet, from hair style, eyebrow shape to sunglass shape. After many years of trials and errors, I settled on a longer, layered hair style that framed my face and softened my jaw line. I learned to avoid square shapes around my face, whether they were square-framed sunglasses or tops with square necklines.

As I made these positive changes, I felt more and more comfortable with my appearance. I started to appreciate my square, angular features, as I realized that they gave me my unique, special look. I also had new perspectives on some of the features that I used to consider especially unattractive. I now view them as assets rather than liabilities.

I was happy with these positive changes, but also regretful that I let so many years pass without making these easy and simple improvements, which many girls already learned as teenagers. I had to joke about myself with a Chinese saying, "There is no ugly woman, only lazy woman." The good news is, I won't live like the lazy woman anymore.

Personality Also Plays a Role

Our non-physical features play a role in our style as well. As we discover our unique personalities, we will be drawn to certain styles that are aligned with our personalities. I ultimately figured out why the "hello kitty" T-shirt that looked great on my college classmates looked so awkward on me. It didn't fit for my personality.

Being an "Idealist," interested in the deepest meaning of life, I was simply not made for the "hello kitty" kind of cuteness. As part of my style transformation, I gradually developed a preference for a simple, uncluttered, clean-lined look, which blended well with my personality as well as complimented my angular facial features.

A New Way of Wardrobe Planning

Understanding basic styling principles is the first step toward developing a uniquely fulfilling personal style. During my style discovery, I made a detailed list of the desired and undesired features for each type of clothing and accessories. For example, crewneck and V-neck T-shirts are most desirable, while boat neck and scoop neck are not. In addition, I made a complete list of every piece I had in my wardrobe, by category, by color and by style.

Between the two lists, I was able to clearly identify the pieces to get rid of such as those with wrong colors, styles or fits; the pieces to acquire such as a casual spring jacket; and the pieces that I had over-stocked, including an abundance of black sweaters. Apparently, I had the tendency to repetitively acquire certain items while perpetually ignoring the need for a few other items. This illustrated another reason why I always had the feeling of "having nothing to wear."

Based on this new wardrobe plan, I built a complete collection of basic, classic, timeless pieces in every category. In this "baseline" collection, I made sure that I was precise about quality and fit. The fit is critical, especially for some classic, seemingly simple pieces such as a black sheath dress or a pair of slim ankle pants. Two black sheath dresses from different brands may look very similar on the hangers, but there can be a huge difference in terms of how they fit and flow. Wearing ill-fitting clothes for many years, I was absolutely amazed by what a difference the right fit could make.

Wardrobe planning has become an important habit that helps me achieve a well-functioning closet that is both "little waste," and always "having something to wear." It eliminates the many kinds of mistakes I used to make during impulsive shopping. I also feel less compelled to acquire a pile of new clothes every season.

For most of us, our style choices are somewhat limited by what the fashion industry offers. In some seasons, I could hardly find any pieces because the styles that were trendy and fashionable didn't work for me. Because I had my "baseline" wardrobe, I simply chose not to buy or buy less during the season. I still shop spontaneously, based on the wardrobe plan stored in my mind, but I no longer shop impulsively and carelessly.

Style development is an ongoing process. Our style evolves over time. Our physical features, such as our shape and size, may also change with time. However, the principles are the same: identifying our unique features, appreciating our unique features and making the best out of our unique features.

We Are All Beautiful, in Our Unique Ways

Like every flower, each of us has our unique beauty. Our mission is to find the key to unlock our unique beauty. To me, the key is a complimentary personal style combined with beautiful inner qualities and positive attitudes, which can all be cultivated in life.

Self-confidence creates a special charm which makes one more attractive and inviting. With powerful self-confidence, the looks that do not conform to the cultural standard can exude a special beauty and, surprisingly, create a stronger and longer lasting impression. As the singer Taylor Swift said, "Unique and different is the new generation of beautiful."

Chinese super model, Lu Yan, has a look that can hardly be viewed as beautiful based on either eastern or western standards. She has very small eyes that appear to be almost set in a straight line. She also has many freckles on her face. However, with her highly recognizable look and her attitude, she exudes a special kind of beauty. People remember her more than they remember some actresses and models who have been enhanced by cosmetic surgeries according to popular beauty standards. Beauty, as with anything else, loses certain charm once it becomes generic.

Today, I am genuinely content with my look. Even if I could, I wouldn't want to trade it with anyone else because it's the one and only in the world. So is yours. A precious lesson I have learned during this journey is not to focus on our blemishes or shortcomings, but to relish our blessings and gifts. It is fun and exciting to transform our outer style, to cultivate our inner qualities, and to become more beautiful, according to our design and regardless of age.

15

Becoming Your Best Self

*Success comes from knowing that you did your best to
become the best that you are capable of becoming.*
—*John Wooden*

A true sense of individual uniqueness is about recognizing
our unique traits and intrinsic desires, and consciously
developing ourselves and transforming ourselves to become
our own best possible version.

I love this quote which I came across online: "Being the
best is great, you're the number one. Being unique is
greater, you're the only one." I would add that, being unique
and being the best—the best of the unique you—is the
greatest, since you have the opportunity to be both the
"number one" and the "only one."

Being Unique Is Not "Appearing" Different

First and foremost, individual uniqueness is not about
making oneself "appear" different in extrinsic ways. Some
people may attempt to hide a fragile self-image by trying to
appear different and special, such as by carrying an
unconventional look, showing off a certain kind of lifestyle

or displaying pride and disdain toward others. There's a critical difference between trying to prove yourself to the world in order to make up for inadequate self-esteem, and seeking to become the best version of yourself in order to live for the pure exhilaration of excellence.

The need to prove your worth is characterized by anxiety and stress. The desire to express your unique self is characterized by joy and excitement. Ask yourself these questions: Do you constantly feel you must prove your worth with external achievements? Is making an impression more important than being true to yourself? Are the trappings of your lifestyle more important to you than your inner joy?

More than "Just Being Myself"

Simone Biles, the amazing young gymnast and 2016 Olympic gold medalist, once visited our church. As I watched the interview, I was impressed with how she appreciated her unique self and brought out the best of her unique self. When she was asked how she felt about her masculine figure, she said with her lovely, confident smile, "I enjoy being myself."

On our way home, my daughter and I had a conversation about some of the behaviors I would like for her to improve. She smiled and responded, "I am just being myself, mom. Simone Biles just said we should enjoy being ourselves." I knew from her smile that she was just joking with me. Still, I couldn't help wondering how many adults and children have distorted the meaning of "just being myself." When we hold on to bad habits, attitudes and refuse to improve ourselves, the rationale of "just being myself," may be expressed more honestly as "just harming myself."

No matter how unique each of us is, we all need to follow some basic guidelines in life. Be different, if it means higher personal and professional standards. Be different, if it means being more gracious and considerate to others. Be different, if it means putting more time and effort into every worthy cause to which we are committed.

Develop Authentic Self-esteem

A deep, thorough awareness of our individual uniqueness places us in the right position in the universe, and transforms the way we view ourselves and others. It gives us genuine confidence and at the same time humbles us. We don't feel inferior to others because there is a unique purpose and plan for us. We don't feel superior to others either because recognizing our uniqueness also means recognizing others' uniqueness. We begin to see people as being special and different from each other, instead of being better or worse than each other.

As a result, comparing ourselves to others is neither necessary nor meaningful. As we shift our focus to everyone's unique, intrinsic values, it becomes easier to truly love ourselves and genuinely appreciate others. Accordingly, we are able to develop authentic self-esteem and harmonious relationships with ourselves, with others, and with the universe itself.

Comparing ourselves to others is a frustrating experience that virtually all people go through in life. The less we recognize our intrinsic values, the more likely we are to compare ourselves to others, based on outer factors such as money, looks, status, and accomplishments.

If we are doing well, the comparison may temporarily work in our favor and makes us feel superior and inflated. However, we will soon discover that there are individuals and families doing better than we are. Ultimately, this never-ending cycle of comparison always leads to self-doubt and make us feel insecure.

Comparison keeps our focus on the negatives, distorts our sense of reality, and damages our self-esteem and relationships with others. It's impossible to love ourselves when we constantly live by comparison. Before I recognized my intrinsic values, I compared myself to the wives who make a "Martha Stewart" home. I compared myself to the moms who offer their children different breakfast options every morning, arranged with the look of various cute animals such as a teddy bear. I compared myself to the classmates who are Wall Street finance experts or top corporate executives. Wherever I compared, I felt inadequate in some way.

As I began my self-discovery, I realized that the value I could offer was different from the value other people could offer because our gifts were different, and that success for me was different from the success for others because our callings were different.

I can't offer my family a "Martha Stewart" home, but I can offer my family a warm and positive atmosphere, plus a decently functional home. I can't offer my children the teddy bear looking breakfast, but I can offer them deep understanding and emotional support, and I can, at least, carve a smiling face in their bread. I can't be a finance expert on Wall Street, but I can help others grow and fulfill their potential through my unique gifts.

As I no longer felt the urge to compare myself to others, I developed a deep sense of personal value and security. I began to genuinely appreciate who I am instead of doubting myself based on how I performed against others. As I became better at recognizing and appreciating my own strengths, I also became better at recognizing and appreciating others' strengths.

Many people live with either low self-esteem or self-inflated pride, because they focus on either their own ineptitudes or others' ineptitudes, instead of everyone's aptitudes. They lose sight of the reality that each individual is a holistic creation with their unique strengths along with their unique limitations.

Comparing ourselves to others makes us feel insecure and self-conscious. The same applies when comparing ourselves to societal and cultural standards. In traditional Asian aesthetics, a beautiful woman is supposed to have a soft, oval shaped face, narrow jaws, high nose bridge, and large eyes with double eyelids.

Many Asian women rush to Korea, the hot spot for cosmetic surgeries, to reshape themselves to these standards. Common procedures include creating double eyelids, raising nose bridges, and shaving jaw bones in order to narrow the jaws. All of these procedures involve some level of risk. Jaw reduction can be particularly dangerous as it may cause complications such as chronic jaw pain, skewed mouth, misaligned teeth and even the inability to chew or smile.

Several years ago, a 23-year-old Korean woman took her own life after having double jaw reduction surgery. She left a note explaining her desperation after the surgery that had left her unable to chew food, and unable to stop crying due to nerve damage in a tear duct. Behind the heartbreaking story is the painful reality that many people don't love themselves because of the perceived imperfections in how they look.

Before my self-discovery, I never considered myself beautiful because of my square, angular face, and my average-sized eyes framed with single eye lids. I secretly wished I could have a narrower jaw, bigger eyes and a softer look. It wasn't until I recognized my own uniqueness that I began to embrace and love these features.

"Personality begins where comparison ends," said the fashion designer Karl Lagerfeld. Accepting ourselves as we are is the most critical aspect in developing authentic self-esteem and belief in our potential. As we accept our features, both inner and outer, as integral parts of our holistic self, our unique personality will begin to emerge and begin to shine. We will begin to truly appreciate and love ourselves.

Cultivate an Abundance Mindset

Belief creates reality. Having an abundance mindset as opposed to a scarcity mindset has a profound impact on how we lead our lives and what we can achieve in life.

The essence of the scarcity mindset is that there are only limited resources and opportunities in the world. This belief leads people to feel that they must hoard, guard, or constantly protect their possessions, and they need to compete for their share of the limited resources.

Many people struggle with a scarcity mindset throughout their lives. Some constantly worry about job security. Some get into vicious competition for a small raise or promotion. Some are always jealous of others' accomplishments. It's difficult for them to share knowledge, credit or resources, as well as feel genuinely happy for the good things happening to others. People with a scarcity mindset tend to live with the inner pain of inadequacy, sadness, jealousy, and anger. Their belief in scarcity often leads to a reality of scarcity, as reflected in poor finance, stagnant life goals and strained relationships with others.

People with a scarcity mindset are confined by their circumstances and miss seeing the infinite possibilities for solving problems, sharing goals, and creating opportunities. It's easy to fall into the trap of the scarcity mindset when we see ourselves as generic versions of human beings, almost like commodities. Because we fail to recognize the full spectrum of our unique gifts and potential, we become oblivious to the many pathways through which we may excel in life. As a result, it seems like the only way to survive is to compete on a single, narrow path.

When I conducted trainings on this topic, some people argued that many situations in life called for competition, and it was impossible not to have the scarcity mindset. Competition is not necessarily a bad thing. As I tell my daughters, competition is good when the focus is to improve ourselves. It tells us where we are and motivates us to bring out the best in us. It only turns bad when we allow competition to dictate our values, limit our views, and even worse, turn us against others.

The key question is, does an individual have to be defined and confined by competition on a single, narrow path? Vera Wang, a distinguished fashion designer, was previously a promising figure skater who competed at the level of U.S. Figure Skating Championships. Unfortunately, she failed to qualify for the Olympic team. She left her skating career and entered the fashion industry instead. However, her passion for skating didn't end there. Forty years later, she was inducted into the U.S. Figure Skating Hall of Fame, not for her accomplishment as a skater, but for her contribution to the sport as a costume designer.

As author Marianne Williamson noted, "The key to abundance is meeting limited circumstances with unlimited thoughts." As we begin to recognize our unique gifts and potential, we will be able to broaden our vision and see the big picture of life beyond our circumstances. We will be able to see possibilities, alternatives and options that we otherwise wouldn't have seen. We will be able to create opportunities that we otherwise wouldn't be able to create. Through these observations, we are able to cultivate an abundance mindset.

An abundance mindset recognizes that there are abundant resources and opportunities in the world, more than one will ever need. People with an abundance mindset are open, creative, willing to share and cooperate. While a business executive with a scarcity mindset considers every competitor as his enemy and every win by the competitor as his own loss, one with an abundance mindset focus on sharpening his business's unique value propositions and developing the huge unexplored market which his business is best positioned to serve.

People with an abundance mindset can be genuinely happy about other people's success as they recognize that there are many possibilities, options, alternatives for themselves to succeed. Their belief in abundance often leads to a reality of abundance, as reflected in financial prosperity, fulfilling career and harmonious relationships with others.

Like many people, I used to think my career success solely depended on how far up I could climb on the corporate ladder. This simple, limiting thought made me a victim of the scarcity mindset for many years. Fortunately, through self-discovery, I developed an abundance mindset and realized that climbing the corporate ladder was not my only path to success. I began to see many new possibilities, and also began to attract the resources and opportunities that would move me toward my vision. From this experience, I became keenly aware of the awesome power of the mind.

As I internalized the belief that everyone has a unique, abundant, fulfilling way of living, I began to feel genuinely happy for the accomplishment of others. I enjoyed sharing with others as well as learning from others. I was transformed into an abundance mindset and felt more self-assured than I had ever been.

Great Faith in Great Vision

One of my favorite Bible verses is, "Faith is the substance of things hoped for, the evidence of things not seen." Belief is the key that can unlock the right door for everyone, and the means for getting rid of the mental prison that keeps people from ever knowing success. Belief attracts the right people and opportunities into our lives to form that much-needed bridge between dreams and reality. It's a power that everyone has but few consciously use.

Studies conducted during the past several decades show that science and religion are aligned. It is a spiritual law, proven by quantum physics, that our vision, faith and reality are closely connected. When we are able to see our dreams through our mind's eye, we are much more likely to see them manifested in reality before our physical eyes. Although the popular adage is "never cross a bridge until you come to it," the most successful people in our world had crossed those bridges in their imaginations long before they ever saw them.

From a young age, I intuitively sensed that we had the ability to attract what we genuinely wished for and intensely focused on. "Genuinely" and "intensely" are the key words. I could say that I want to be the best dancer in the world—that would be very nice of course—but it's not going to happen because it's not the deep desire of my heart and it wouldn't trigger serious actions.

During college, the girls in my dorm liked to play a game—every one of us giving a word describing our future husband. Without hesitation, I always gave the word "cooking." My parents were very busy at work as I grew up. They rarely had time to cook anything fancier beyond the basics. As a child, I dreamed of a family life with the rich, warm aroma of food constantly filling the house.

Because I had little experience with cooking, and I was not yet aware of the concept called "self-development," I dreamed of a husband who, on top of other good attributes, would be a good cook. I soon met a boyfriend, now my husband, who loved food and cooking, and of course, had many other good qualities as well. Our dorms didn't have a kitchen, but he loved food so much that he managed to cook using a tiny table stove. Even today, one of his favorite things is to figure out how to replicate the good food he has tasted in a restaurant or in our friends' houses.

It's helpful to reflect your vision on a dream board, the visual representation of goals and dreams, so that you can constantly see it and experience it in your mind. I have learned that only 20% of the population have a dream board and for those with a dream board, 80% of their dreams come true. Although I didn't have a dream board until recent years, I developed the habit of imagining my goals and then writing them down in detailed descriptions, like the descriptions I wrote about my calling.

When you live with intention, a positive and clear expectation about life, you are likely to experience greater success and fulfillment in professional and personal life. People living without intention tend to go through the motions, and very often, are trapped in a busy life that goes nowhere.

We usually have a new vision as result of self-discovery. This is a great starting point since the key to finding what you want is knowing what you want. Sometimes the new vision may be so far away from our current reality that it seems impossible to reach, as it was in my own case. In order to form the bridge, we need hold on to our vision with unwavering faith and pursue it with persistent actions.

As a caveat, some people misinterpret the spiritual law as a shortcut to meet greedy desires with the least amount of effort. The story usually goes like this: "I wrote down on my dream board that I wanted to be a millionaire. I posted it on my refrigerator and I looked at it every day. But years have passed and nothing has happened!"

Nothing has happened and won't happen because a dream without actions is merely empty, wishful thinking. A genuine vision is a laser-sharp picture of the future rooted in a deep desire burning inside. It triggers the most intense and persistent actions.

Move from "Can Not" to "Why Not"

Much has been said about the self-fulfilling prophecy. A self-fulfilling prophecy is a prediction that becomes true because one expects it to be true. Whether you think something is possible or impossible, whether you believe you will succeed or you will fail, the result you get often meets your expectations.

As we work toward our vision, we want to be sensitive to the inspirations and opportunities showing up in our life.

Particularly, we want to respond to them with an open mind and with courage, and never quench them with the thought of "impossible."

I learned the importance of believing in "nothing is impossible" soon after I came to the U.S. I came to the country in 1998 to join my husband, who was pursuing his Ph.D. degree at Drexel University, Philadelphia. It was exciting to experience a new country, but the excitement quickly faded away as reality kicked in.

At the time, our only source of income was my husband's in-school job as a research assistant. It was just enough to pay for rent and food. I hesitated even to buy a five-dollar T-shirt. I wished to re-establish my career but, as I had heard, that would require a working visa, which consequently would require advanced education in U.S. There was no way I could afford that education. As I thought about life for the next five years, anxiety, despair and self-doubt started to take over.

Two months after I came to Philadelphia, I had the opportunity to connect with a group of volunteers who helped foreign students' spouses, like myself, learn English. This was a group of retired ladies living in downtown Philadelphia. Their love, kindness, and hospitality were precious and heartwarming. I was assigned to work with Lilian, who was in her 80s and held a Ph.D. degree in Sociology from the University of Pennsylvania.

Every Tuesday morning, I would walk from my 34th street apartment to her quaint row house not far from the 30th street train station. We usually started by me reading the local newspaper. She would correct my pronunciation in the process. After that, we would chat about everything else in life. Lilian not only helped me improve my English, but also exposed me to many aspects of the U.S. culture.

One day she asked me about my plans for the future. I told her about my situation. She asked, "Why don't you go find a job?" I almost immediately dismissed the idea with a wave of my hand: "Lilian, no, no, that's not possible. I don't have any education or work experience in this country. No one like me has been able to get a job without first going to a school here."

Acting as if she didn't hear me, Lilian walked calmly to her kitchen, bringing a pile of newspapers to me, and said, "Take these. These are the Saturday newspapers from the last few weeks. Go to the employment section and just try it." I thought it would be a waste of time but her confidence was infectious and I didn't want to disappoint her.

I sent out twenty or so resumes during the following week, and I couldn't believe what happened as a result. I got a few responses quickly. One company, after a brief chat, asked me to come to their office in Wilmington, Delaware for a face to face interview. I could hardly wait to report the good news to Lilian. When we met again in her row house, she advised me about the interview, checked what clothing I planned to wear, and loaned me a hand bag to carry for the interview.

With her love and encouragement, I ventured into my first train ride and my first job interview in the U.S. Because I didn't know how to drive yet, the only way to get to the office was to ride a train from Philadelphia's 30th street station to Wilmington station, and then take a ten-minute walk from there to the office.

I carried an umbrella as a storm was forecasted to arrive. The weather man was accurate in this case and the deluge began in full force just as I got off the train. In order to get to the interview on time, I had no choice other than walking directly into it. The rain was pouring down and the umbrella was virtually useless due to the strong wind. By the time I arrived at the Hotel du Pont, where the office was located, my pants were soaking wet below the knees. My hair was wet and messy.

I did my best to collect myself but felt really embarrassed when I walked into the office of Kathleen, the Vice President of Finance. She was a warm and charming lady with sleek short hair. Her welcoming words put me right at ease. The interview went smoothly. She liked the finance experiences I had with the two Fortune 500 companies back in China. She also showed great care by asking me about my three months of experience living in the U.S., and shared her own experience as a mom with children overseas.

What happened next was like a rollercoaster ride. Soon after I got home, I received a call from HR informing me that I was hired. Before I recovered from the excitement, I received another call saying that the company was not able to hire me because of my visa status. On the second day, before I fully processed the sadness and disappointment, I received a third call informing me that the company decided to apply for the working visa for me because of the good match between my experience and the position. I could expect to start after the working visa was approved. I was so excited that I immediately ran to Lilian to report the great news to her.

Six months later, I was on my way to my first job in the U.S. Kathleen trusted me and supported me in my work for the next eight years. My husband and I relocated several times because of his job. Kathleen made sure I had a position when we moved to each new location. In spite of her demanding schedule, she called to wish me a happy birthday every year. It warms my heart whenever I think of her.

I feel a special gratitude to Lilian and Kathleen for believing in me. I also feel a special gratitude to God for leading Lilian and Kathleen into my life and shaping "impossible" situations into "possible" through them.

As we embrace the idea of "nothing is impossible," asking "why not" instead of accepting "can not," our self-fulfilling prophecy will work in our favor and open a new world of opportunities.

For many of us, a few critical turning points in life usually determine the overall course of our life. The details and routines just fill the years in between. I often wonder how beautiful life would be if we could hear a gentle voice at each of the turning points and courageously follow its nudge.

Although not all of us can hear the gentle voice, some people are better than others at recognizing the opportunities in their lives. As I have observed, these individuals tend to be open-minded and decisive. Furthermore, they don't fear judgment or rejections.

Overcome Fear of Judgment and Rejection

Many people, including myself, have missed opportunities in life because of the fear of rejection and fear of appearing foolish in the eyes of others. A career breakthrough, a loving relationship, a life-changing friend, can all be missed if we are paralyzed by fear and hesitation, not acting on the urgings in our hearts.

When I was a student, I sometimes had great ideas when a teacher asked a question. I wanted to share but I always hesitated to raise my hand. By the time I mustered up enough courage to contribute, the teacher already had moved on to other topics. Outside of our classrooms, I often missed opportunities in life because of my insecurities.

Fear of judgment and fear of rejection are two of the toughest obstacles that prevent us from realizing our potential. The more we care about what others think, the more we become insecure, self-conscious, hesitating, and the less we dare to do anything beyond the status quo. We must deal with these fears in order to live a truly free and fulfilling life.

Each of us has our unique journey in terms of how to overcome these fears. I overcame the fear of judgment primarily through my faith. I realized that God is the only one to whom I am ultimately accountable. Like all human beings, I can never be perfect, nor can I remake others into my image of perfection. "He who trims himself to suit everyone will soon whittle himself away," said Canadian playwright Raymond Hull. My mission in life is not to whittle myself away, but to become the best version of myself while approaching people and the world with a good intention and a loving heart.

Each of us is innately different. We also come from different backgrounds, hold different values and have different self-interests. As a result, we view things from different heights and angles. Some people are going to dislike what we do or what we say; some people are going to interpret our words and actions differently from the way they are intended. It's simply a part of life which we need learn to accept with peace.

I used to see the world based on absolutes such as good or bad, right or wrong, true or false. As I became more mature, I was able to comprehend that sometimes there were very few absolutes that apply to every situation. One may think that it's wrong not to tell a patient there is little or no hope of surviving a serious disease, based on statistical facts. Another may think it's best to always offer hope and encouragement. Our version of what's "right or true" is often a matter of our perspectives and philosophies. As writer Anais Nin said, "We don't see things as they are, we see them as we are."

Naturally, as human beings, we tend to like those who think and act like ourselves. If you are becoming different, you should be prepared for the possibility of others around you being uncomfortable with your changes, regardless of how positive they are. You may want to surround yourself with more likeminded people so that they can support you during your transformation.

Concerning the fear of rejection, one of my important lessons learned is that people may reject an idea but not necessarily the person offering the idea. People usually reject an idea because they don't perceive it as a "need or want;" or the timing is wrong for that idea to be considered as a priority. Yet, many of us take these "turn downs" as personal rejections, feeling hurt or holding grudges as a result of these uncomfortable events.

A healthy reaction is to understand and respect others' choices while staying true to our own beliefs, which is the foundation for strong, mature relationships. As Confucius said, "Gentlemen seek harmony but not uniformity."

Physically, we develop stronger muscles as the body repairs damaged tendons and fibers after a strenuous workout or during rehab from an injury. Mentally and emotionally, we revitalize ourselves in a similar way. We acquire resilience by treating each disappointment as a learning experience to help us get wiser and stronger.

You will feel a fresh sense of freedom as you overcome these fears through a series of spiritual, mental and emotional breakthroughs. Many invisible bondages such as these fears keep us imprisoned at the bottom of the mountain. As we climb up the mountain, we have to break out of the bondages, one by one, so that we can walk freely, run freely and then finally, sing freely at the top of the mountain.

Persevere in Your Actions

Our vision often involves long term goals that can only be accomplished with persistent actions. As our dream gets bigger, there will be more hard work, challenges and setbacks. There has to be perseverance in addition to passion in order to sustain the amount of actions required to reach the goals.

Perseverance comes to me partly because of my "futuristic" nature. As a natural tendency, I am future oriented and inspired by the vision of the future. But for the most part, I attribute it to my upbringing. As I grew up, I was taught at school and at home that once we set a goal, we should carry it from beginning to end or to an acceptable level of success. As my dad said, "If you enter a new job, you would not quit in one month just because you are not happy. If you decide to pursue a goal, you would not drop it suddenly just because you have a bad day."

In the past, when I persevered through challenges in life, my inner-dialogue often involved "I was determined," driven by the discipline I had acquired from childhood. After I discovered my passion, my inner-dialogue has evolved to "I was compelled," similar to what Yuriy and Vanessa experienced. When the perseverance was primarily driven by discipline, it felt like something forced from the outside, painful and boring. However, when the perseverance was primarily driven by passion, it felt like something inspired from within, enthusiastic and exciting.

Admittedly, before my self-discovery, there were times in life when my discipline led me to persevere in the wrong direction. But if I had to choose again, I would rather have the discipline and make a few detours, than not have the discipline and accomplish little in life.

Passion, perseverance and resilience are key attributes to achieve our dreams. Successful people are continuously pursuing, learning, doing, and overcoming; not merely "trying." Some people say "I will try" when they decide to pursue their dreams. "I will try" is one of the most failure predicting phrases, because it implies giving up at the first few signs of challenges. Every time I hear that phrase, I can't help thinking of Yoda's wise words in the movie *Star Wars*, "Do. Or do not. There is no try."

No matter what "hardware" with which you are blessed, you have the power to write your own "software"—your knowledge, skills, characters, values, attitudes, and mindset. It's your "software" that determines to what extent you can make use of your "hardware." Be your own author. Write the best "software" for your unique "hardware."

16

Living with Theme and Flame

Everyone needs a theme song!
—*Zooey Deschanel*

The journey of self-discovery and self-transformation is a continuous and ever-evolving process. It may seem to involve quite a bit of work, but the work feels like play because it is exciting to learn about yourself and learn to be yourself. I have shared with you the approaches, tools, and resources that were most helpful to me through my own experiences. Hopefully, you are able to leverage what I have shared and take a shortcut as you set out to discover your unique self.

The traits we have covered, such as temperament, natural talents, passions, values and physical traits, impact many aspects of our lives beyond our calling, health and personal style. Depending on your goals and priorities, you can explore how to express your unique self in more areas such as parenting, relationships, leadership and other aspects of lifestyles. I too have been expanding my interests into more areas as time goes on.

Living by our unique design has a profound impact on our spiritual, mental and physical well-being. Wherever you are in your quest, regardless of your current circumstances and past challenges, I urge you to continue to seek your essence, fulfill your dreams and search for excellence and self-actualization.

Perhaps you are at a turning point in your life, as I was on that cold December day in 2009, after the commencement ceremony when I received my MBA. What should have been a time for celebration became a moment of truth—I had never felt truly fulfilled in spite of all that I had accomplished.

Perhaps you have a few important questions to answer before you move to the next big thing, as I had my three big questions: What should I do in life? How do I live a healthy life? How do I transform my personal style?

Perhaps you have been putting your dreams on hold as I did many years ago. You may have felt that sparkle in your heart but have not acted upon your deepest intuition to ignite the torch within.

Or, perhaps you are one of the lucky few—you are already on your chosen path; you are comfortable with your health; and you feel positive about the reflection you see in the mirror.

No matter what your situation is, I believe you will be inspired as you unlock your inner treasure chests filled with natural gifts that you never realized were there in abundance. It is not what we have done that makes us successful. It is what we are continuing to do each day with what we have learned.

The most significant takeaway from the book is that you are uniquely made, out of the seven billion people who live on earth today. "Know thyself" is the ultimate enlightenment. The more self-knowledge you have, the more power you have to live a truly rewarding life. While recognizing your limitations, the key to fulfillment is to concentrate on your strengths. This will take you as far and as high as you dare to dream.

You want to find your compelling "why" in life which is rooted in who you are and what you truly want from life, much like the strategy for a business. This powerful "why" enables you to live your life with a proactive, strategic and long-term oriented approach, instead of a reactive, tactical and short-term oriented approach.

Your temperament and your natural talents are given. As much as possible, you want to take advantage of these natural gifts, fly with the wind and not against the wind. However, always recognize that there is a tremendous amount of untapped potential within you. You can get better at everything when there is a genuine desire and commitment. When your own talents are not enough, you can accomplish great missions by cultivating "mega talent"—the talent of leveraging and collaborating with others' talents.

Your passion is your fuel to greatness and your vital energy of life. Whether you are passionate about an activity, an opportunity or a mission, take "the road less travelled" and chase your passion, not your pension.

Your values form your inner compass and your unique definition of success. You want to cultivate and follow the values that are most conducive to your happiness and well-being, and pursue success according to your own definition. You may have to "unlearn" some of the old values influenced by your environment before you embrace the new values genuinely important to you.

Your health is your greatest wealth. Nothing is more vital than living a healthy life, because health is the foundation of freedom and it affects everything else you do in life. Be aware of your own health philosophy and develop a personalized healthy lifestyle based on your unique physical characteristics. Take charge of your health as it is your one and only transportation vehicle for the entire life journey.

Your personal style projects you to the world. A clean, polished, confident look that expresses your unique self makes you comfortable in your own skin and helps you project optimism concerning your potential. If, like me, you were born with a look that doesn't conform to popular beauty standards, know that "being unique and different is the new generation of beautiful."

Always keep in mind that, no matter what "hardware" with which you are blessed, you are the author of your "software." It's your unique "software" that determines to what extent you can make the best use of your unique "hardware."

At its very core, this is a book about personalization and differentiation. Being able to personalize your work and lifestyle choices, based on your unique characteristics and intrinsic desires, is the key to a genuinely fulfilling life. Being able to differentiate yourself, with your unique, authentic, hard-to-replicate competencies, is the source of a powerful competitive advantage, especially in a technology-driven world where the competition between humans and machines has been rapidly permeating every sector.

Self-discovery and self-transformation are among the best actions I have taken in my life. Through these actions, I regained my individuality which faded into conformity many years ago. Since embarking on this incredible journey, I have designed my life around one theme: *who I am as a unique individual.* All of my major decisions and actions have been aligned with this one theme. I have experienced a new way of living, constantly making fresh and exciting discoveries.

When you embrace the theme of the "unique you," you will live with clarity and focus.

Instead of sailing like a rudderless ship trying to reach some vague port of call, you will be sailing with a compass, toward a definite port of call. You will experience fewer inner debates, less self-doubt, and have more peace and joy. Most people don't live in peace and joy because, consciously or unconsciously, they live in a way conflicting with their inner self.

The more self-knowledge I have, the more intuitive, confident and assured I become. I am able to quickly distinguish the signals aligned with the "unique me" and filter out the noises misaligned with the "unique me," whether they are popular standards, people's opinions, judgments or misjudgments. I become more in tune with opportunities as well as more cognizant of distractions.

Clarity leads to focus. A common reason for business and personal failure is a lack of focus. Success is often not about addition but about subtraction. You have to prune a tree, getting rid of all the unnecessary branches and stems, in order for the tree to grow strong and fruitful. A lot of wisdom gained in life is about what "not" to do.

Focus is so powerful that you can ignite a piece of paper with sunlight focused on it through a small magnifying glass. When you concentrate your energy like a laser beam, you are on the most effective and least resistant track to accomplish your dreams, because focus creates the strongest momentum.

I used to be committed to many scattered activities, which didn't take me far in spite of my busyness. This changed completely as I became focused on the theme of the "unique me." The more answers I found to my basic three questions, the more I experienced a sense of synergy between my actions and decisions. There also seems to be a compound effect—a series of small, coherent actions that build upon each other can accomplish a surprisingly large result.

Things have become so much easier now as I consistently focus on my core passions and values rather than chase the popular "menus of the day."

When you internalize the theme of the "unique you," you will live with simplicity.

As Leonardo da Vinci said, "Simplicity is the ultimate sophistication." It's stressful to live in a world where we are bombarded by an overwhelming amount of stuff and information. In recent years, minimalist living has attracted a lot of interest, for good reasons. Although I am not a diehard minimalist yet, with a heightened awareness on what's truly essential, I have been able to reduce all forms of unnecessities and waste.

I become more precise in what I like and what I need in terms of all material belongings. Similar to what I did with my wardrobe planning, before bringing any items into the house—expensive, inexpensive or free—I make sure that I like them and will use them. I am also instilling in my children that, money is better used to create beautiful experiences and unforgettable memories than unnecessary material possessions.

I am less engaged in activities that I now consider as a waste of time, such as aimlessly spending hours and hours in front of the TV or Internet screen. Knowing my own passions, I prefer to focus on living my own life story. While I enjoy learning from positive role models, I want to be in the arena of life, fully engaged as a participant, rather than be a spectator in the audience.

With less exposure to media, surprisingly, I am not missing anything truly interesting, important or life altering. I still have access to important news, insightful articles and wonderful shows through other channels, not the least of which has been word of mouth.

I find myself detached more and more from mental waste, characterized by negative, non-productive thoughts. Spiritually, knowing I am unique at a personal level makes me feel a deeper sense of love, gratitude, security and a greater appreciation for everyone and everything in my life. My new spiritual reality has gradually manifested into a new physical reality.

By holding simple and positive thoughts, my life has been simplified; my creativity has been expanded; my mind has been opened to the authentic beauty surrounding us, simple pleasures becoming exquisite treasures. I have also been blessed with many positive and supportive people in my life.

Of course, we all encounter people who may seem challenging and difficult. However, as delivered so well in one of my favorite songs from the musical *Wicked*, "I have heard that people come into our life for a reason, bringing something we must learn. And we are led to those who help us most to grow, if we let them, and we help them in return."

When you transform yourself according to the theme of the "unique you," you will live with flame—a constant inner glow of joy and enthusiasm.

I have observed many people who live with theme and flame. Some are young college students. Fresh and innocent, they are just setting out to pursue their dreams and explore what life has to offer. Some are already in their golden years. Mature and sophisticated, they have walked through the mountains and valleys in life and seen the depth and breadth of human nature. Regardless of how old they are and what their stories may be, they all share one thing in common: a bright, passionate and young heart. One word keeps coming to my mind to describe them. The word is "ageless."

May you be blessed with being ageless, forever living with theme and flame.

Epilogue

The girl from China, now a grown woman, is sitting quietly in a tree-studded park, not far from her home in the northern suburbs of Chicago. She smiles as she hears the laughter of her two daughters playing with friends on this lovely spring afternoon. Content and totally immersed in the environment, she notices a beautiful Monarch butterfly fluttering close overhead.

The butterfly appears unconcerned and comfortable in being very near, landing gently on a flower growing only a few feet away from the park bench. The exquisite butterfly seems to have a special persona, as if it somehow senses its own destination and destiny, pausing only briefly to drink the sweet nectar from the blossom, before continuing on its journey.

After resting and refreshing, it glides gently away, circling higher and higher, above the woman's head before finally disappearing from view. The interlude seems significant and perhaps a special sign of some kind of liberation.

The woman turns her attention back to the trees, flowers, the sun, the gentle breeze and the joyful sounds of the children playing. For a moment, her thoughts travel back to her carefree childhood and all of the twists and turns her life had taken through the years. The past has become a collection of learning experiences and rich, indelible memories... The future, a mysterious chrysalis, is not yet ready to be opened.

Savoring this present moment, she understands who she is becoming.

References

3. Looking Behind the Mirror
Sinek, Simon. "How Great Leaders Inspire Action." *Simon Sinek: How Great Leaders Inspire Action | TED Talk*, www.ted.com/talks/simon_sinek_how_great_leaders _inspire_action.
"Dunning–Kruger Effect." *Wikipedia*, Wikimedia Foundation, 30 Sept. 2017, en.wikipedia.org/wiki/Dunning%E2%80%93Kruger_e ffect.

4. Your Temperament is Permanent
Keirsey, David. *Please Understand Me II: Temperament, Character, Intelligence.* Topeka Bindery, 2009.
"Personality Test - Keirsey Temperament Website." *Personality Test - Keirsey Temperament Website*, www.keirsey.com/.
"The Myers & Briggs Foundation." *The Myers & Briggs Foundation*, www.myersbriggs.org/.
"DiSC Profile - Learn about Yourself. Work More Productively." *DiSCProfile.com*, www.DiSCProfile.com/.
"Mere-Exposure Effect." *Wikipedia*, Wikimedia Foundation, 16 Aug. 2017, en.wikipedia.org/wiki/Mere-exposure_effect.
"Production Blocking." *Wikipedia*, Wikimedia Foundation, 13 Sept. 2017, en.wikipedia.org/wiki/Production_blocking.
Cain, Susan. *Quiet: the Power of Introverts in a World That Can't Stop Speaking.* Center Point Publishing, 2012.

5. Your Priceless Natural Talents
Csikszentmihalyi, Mihaly. *Flow: the Psychology of Optimal Experience.* Harper Perennial Modern Classics, 2008

"Aptitude Testing and Research since 1922." *Johnson O'Connor Research Foundation*, www.jocrf.org/.

"Our Book: Understanding Your Aptitudes." *Johnson O'Connor Research Foundation*, www.jocrf.org/aptitudes/book-understanding-your-aptitudes.

"The Ball Foundation." *The Ball Foundation*, www.ballfoundation.org.

"CliftonStrengths Solutions." *CliftonStrengths Solutions*, www.gallupstrengthscenter.com/.

Gardner, Howard. *Frames of Mind: The Theory of Multiple Intelligences*. Basic Books, 2011.

Arbesman, Samuel. "Be Forewarned: Your Knowledge Is Decaying." Harvard Business Review, 7 Aug. 2014, hbr.org/2012/11/be-forewarned-your-knowledge-i.

"Knowledge Doubling Every 12 Months, Soon to Be Every 12 Hours." Industry Tap, 19 Apr. 2013, www.industrytap.com/knowledge-doubling-every-12-months-soon-to-be-every-12-hours/3950.

McCuen@aacu.org. "It Takes More than a Major: Employer Priorities for College Learning and Student Success: Overview and Key Findings." Association of American Colleges & Universities, 22 Feb. 2016, www.aacu.org/leap/presidentstrust/compact/2013Sur veySummary.

7. Values: The Guiding Lights

"Rokeach Value Survey." *Wikipedia*, Wikimedia Foundation, 24 Nov. 2016, en.wikipedia.org/wiki/Rokeach_Value_Survey.

"Universal Value." *Wikipedia*, Wikimedia Foundation, 30 Sept. 2017, en.wikipedia.org/wiki/Universal_value.

Walton, Alice G. "Why The Super-Successful Get Depressed." Forbes. 06 Feb. 2015, https://www.forbes.com/sites/alicegwalton/2015/01/2 6/why-the-super-successful-get-depressed/

8. Taking the Road Less Travelled

Peck, Morgan Scott. *The Road Less Travelled*. Touchstone, 2003.

"Automation and Anxiety." *The Economist*, The Economist Newspaper, 25 June 2016, www.economist.com/news/special-report/21700758-will-smarter-machines-cause-mass-unemployment-automation-and-anxiety

"The Workforce of the Future Will Be Increasingly Flexible." Workforce 2020. N.p., 17 Sept. 2014.

"Loss Aversion." *Wikipedia*, Wikimedia Foundation, 7 Sept. 2017, en.wikipedia.org/wiki/Loss_aversion.

Chopra, Deepak. *The Seven Spiritual Laws of Success*. Amber-Allen Publishing, 2015.

9. Children Have Their Own Destinies

Gibran, Kahlil. *The Prophet*. Alfred A. Knopf, 1923.

Chua, Amy. *Battle Hymn of the Tiger Mother*. Bloomsbury Publishing, 2014.

10. What Is Your Health Philosophy?

"Disease-Prone and Self-Healing Personalities." *Psychiatric Services*, ps.psychiatryonline.org/doi/abs/10.1176/ps.43.12.1177?journalCode=ps.

"Morita Therapy." *Wikipedia*, Wikimedia Foundation, 22 Aug. 2017, en.wikipedia.org/wiki/Morita_therapy.

11. Ideal Diet: The Diet That Is Right for You

D'Adamo, Peter, and Catherine Whitney. *Eat Right 4 Your Type: the Individualized Blood Type Diet Solution*. Berkley, 2016.

"Eat Right for Your Metabolism Type." *The Dr. Oz Show*, The Dr. Oz Show, 16 Sept. 2012, www.doctoroz.com/article/your-metabolism-type-diet.

Price, Weston Andrew. *Nutrition and Physical Degeneration.* Price Pottenger Nutrition, 2008.

12. Nutritional Supplementation: When Food Is Not Enough

Strand, Ray D., and Donna K. Wallace. *What Your Doctor Doesn't Know about Nutritional Medicine May Be Killing You.* Thomas Nelson, 2013.

MacWilliam, Lyle. *NutriSearch Comparative Guide to Nutritional Supplements for the Americas (6th Edition).* NutriSearch Corporation, 2017.

Jensen, Bernard, and Mark Anderson. *Empty Harvest: Understanding the Link between Our Food, Our Immunity, and Our Planet.* Avery, 1995.

"Food Nutrition Has Been Declining! Minerals Go Down, Disease Goes Up." *Nutrition Security Institute,* www.nutritionsecurity.org/.

MSc, Robert H. Fletcher MD. "Vitamins for Chronic Disease Prevention in Adults." *JAMA,* American Medical Association, 19 June 2002, jamanetwork.com/journals/jama/fullarticle/195039.

"Dietary Supplement Health and Education Act of 1994." *Wikipedia,* Wikimedia Foundation, 1 Oct. 2017, en.wikipedia.org/wiki/Dietary_Supplement_Health_a nd_Education_Act_of_1994.

13. Your Exercise, Your Day

Davies, K J. "Oxidative Stress: the Paradox of Aerobic Life." *Biochemical Society Symposium.,* U.S. National Library of Medicine, www.ncbi.nlm.nih.gov/pubmed/8660387.

Smolensky, Michael H., and Lynne Lamberg. *The Body Clock Guide to Better Health: How to Use Your Body's Natural Clock to Fight Illness and Achieve Maximum Health.* H. Holt, 2001.

"Tracking Patients' Circadian Rhythm Could Improve Cancer Treatment." Horizon: the EU Research & Innovation Magazine, horizon-magazine.eu/article/chemotherapy-could-work-twice-well-if-given-right-time_en.html.

14. Projecting Your Unique Style

Horan, Sean M. "The Extraordinary Importance of First Impressions." Psychology Today. Sussex Publishers, 18 Oct. 2014, https://www.psychologytoday.com/blog/adventures-in-dating/201410/the-extraordinary-importance-first-impressions.

Farr, Kendall. *The Pocket Stylist: Behind the Scenes Expertise from a Fashion pro on Creating Your Own Look.* Avery, 2004.

Jackson, Carole. *Color Me Beautiful: Discover Your Natural Beauty Through the Colors That Make You Look Great and Feel Fabulous.* Ballantine Books, 1987.

About the Author

Lydia Wei was born in China and moved to the United States in 1998. She has held finance and pricing management roles in several global companies, including prominent Fortune 500 corporations.

Led by her self-discovery, she became a DDI Certified Facilitator, and has since helped others reach their potential through training, coaching and speaking. Communicating fluently in English and Chinese, she has worked with audiences in the United States and in Asia. Lydia believes that personalization and differentiation, based on a deep understanding of individual uniqueness, are the keys to a genuinely fulfilling life and the sources of a powerful competitive advantage. She is also a passionate advocate for living a life of health and freedom.

Lydia has an MBA from the University of Chicago Booth School of Business, with concentrations in Economics and Management & Organizational Behavior. She also has a master's degree in Information Systems from Drexel University and a bachelor's degree in Economics from Nankai University in China. She lives in the greater Chicago area with her family.

Lydia can be contacted via email:
Lydiawei10@gmail.com